C000131395

WILDFOWLING

By

C. T. DALGETY

LONDON

PHILIP ALLAN

69 GREAT RUSSELL STREET

CONTENTS

ILLUSTRATIONS

IN THE TEXT

CHAPTER I

SHOULDER GUNS, ETC.

The gun is the most important item of a wildfowler's outfit, and should receive more consideration than it often gets. Under the heading of wildfowling are many different forms of shooting; the ideal gun for one may be most unsuitable for another. Thus a four-bore may be suitable for a strong man, flighting geese in a place where they are much shot at; but the lightest and handiest of twelve-bores is best for flighting wigeon where they come to their feeding grounds when it is almost dark.

I have found a twelve-bore chambered for 3 in cartridges to be much the most suitable weapon for all round wildfowling. A double-barrelled four-bore or eight-bore is much too heavy to carry any distance. It is quite impossible to take snap shots with it (though I have shot snipe with an eight-bore), and it is almost impossible to swing with it. A ten-bore is as good as a 3 in twelve-bore, except that it is often impossible to get cartridges for it. Those who find a 3 in twelve-bore too heavy, or who cannot afford to get one, need have no fears of going out with the ordinary gun they use for game shooting.

I will now describe my own gun and state what I consider to be its advantages. It is a twelve-bore, chambered for 3 in cases ; weight, 7¾ lb ; length of barrel, 30 inches. The rib is serrated. The safety catch is in the usual place on the top of the front of the grip, just behind the lever for opening the gun.

Wherever it is possible to buy a cartridge, in the British Isles, twelve-bore cartridges are procurable. So, if I run out of ammunition, I can always get some kind of cartridge to fire from this gun. 2½ in cartridges are not so powerful as 3 in ones, but they will do for all normal ranges.

The weight of 7¾ lb I like because it is not too heavy for carrying about, or for quick shooting, and it is not so light that I feel the recoil unpleasantly.

The 30 in barrels are long enough for slow burning powders such as Amberite and modified Smokeless Diamond. If the barrels were shorter I should be seriously incommoded by the flash, when shooting in the dusk. Also, I personally find it easier to shoot straight with a long barrel.

The serrated rib enables me to see my barrels when aiming at the sky or water in the dark. A plain rib, like the barrels, reflects the sky and becomes quite invisible; while a serrated rib appears black, owing to the dark shadow on each of the little ridges.

The movement of my thumb to the top lever and top safety catch comes more naturally to me than that required for any other type of lever or safety catch. I find the safety catch on the side of a gun most difficult to put up quickly. Also it is usually in a recess which is apt to get filled with mud or sand which puts it out of action.

My gun is hammerless, but is not an ejector. The advantages of a hammerless gun are too obvious to need recounting here. Ejectors for 3 in cartridges are not always satisfactory. A little mud or damp on the cartridge case and it fails to eject. An uncertain ejector is far more nuisance than a non-ejector, so it is important to make sure that the ejector-springs are powerful enough to throw a 3 in case well clear of the breech.

A new gun, like that described above, will cost about £14. There is no object in paying much more. A wildfowling gun cannot be cared for in the same way as a game-shooting gun. It is bound to get much ill treatment: scratches and knocks and corrosion from salt water. Engraving and other external beautifications are wasted on a gun of this type.

In choosing a new gun, the pattern should be tried with a size of shot which is suited to the intended quarry. No two barrels made on the same machine will throw the same pattern, and a gun which throws a good pattern with one size of shot, will not always do so with another size.

When I bought the gun which I use now, I took five guns which were made on the same machine and tested their patterns on the plates. Two of the five were ruled out at once, for throwing too wide a pattern. One of the remaining three threw a hopelessly bad pattern with both BB and 1. The remaining two both made good patterns with BB, but only one of them made a really good pattern with No. 4. This is the gun which I bought.

Balance is very important: snap shots cannot be made with an ill-balanced gun. The stock of course should be made to fit, and most gun-makers will do the necessary alteration free of charge when the gun is bought from them. Personally I cannot see any object in having a short stock, as is sometimes advised. It is said to be easier to shoot with from a lying or sitting position; but a lying pit should be made so that shots are taken to the left front, when an ordinary stock is the best.

Having chosen a gun with good balance, that

fits you, and throws a good pattern with No. 4 or 5 for ducks, and BB or No. 1 for geese, there are a few other details to consider. The safety catch should be really rough or have some definite knob on it to prevent the thumb slipping. My thumb has often been so cold and devoid of feeling that I have had to push up the safety catch with my thumb nail; there is no remedy for this state of affairs; but a really rough safety catch is a great help when one's thumb is merely numb with cold.

Fittings for a sling on stock and barrel are very useful but are, unfortunately, considered rather unsightly in this country. A piece of cord, without any fittings, can always be used as a sling when required, but it must be taken off before shooting. If the gun is to be used in hot weather, when only a shirt is worn, or even less, a rubber butt plate is advisable. The wooden butt feels extremely hard after a few shots have been fired when only a thin shirt is worn.

Next, after the gun, comes ammunition. In my 3 in chambered gun I always use 3 in cartridges for wildfowling. Many shots are taken at long range, so the cartridges must be adapted for long range, but will be as good as any others at short range. Firstly it must be remembered that large shot has greater striking force at long ranges, but small shot gives a greater number of

pellets in the charge. To take two extremes :
a cartridge loaded with SSG is fired at a duck
at forty yards, from a full choke barrel. There are
twenty-three pellets in the charge, sixteen of
these (70 per cent) go into a circle of 30 in
diameter at the forty yards' range. But the
duck only occupies about one-fourteenth part
of the circle, so the chances are that only one pellet
will hit the whole duck and this is most unlikely
to hit it in a vital spot. Obviously SSG is no good
for duck shooting. Another cartridge, loaded
with No. 10 shot, is fired at the same target
at the same range and from the same barrel.
This time there are 1,275 pellets in the charge,
872 of them go into the 30 in circle and the duck
is plastered with sixty-two of them. But a ' ten '
pellet is so light that at forty yards it has not
enough penetration to reach the vital places of
a duck. This experiment, like most wildfowling
experiments, will teach the fowl something if it
does not teach the fowler.

Now, having found that SSG is much too
large and No. 10 is much too small, we must look
for something in between. BB or No. 1 give a
sufficiency of pellets for hitting a goose in
a vital place at forty yards, and they have sufficient
penetration for some of them to go right through
a goose at that range. But put that same pattern
round a wigeon or a teal and it is soon apparent

that a greater number of pellets are necessary in order to get a close enough pattern to be certain of hitting the bird in a vital place. 'Fours' or 'fives' will meet these requirements and still be heavy enough to have the needed penetration.

Personally I am quite incapable of deliberately trying to shoot at a goose's head; I always shoot at the goose. Were I sufficiently cool, calm, and collected and a good enough shot, I should never use shot larger than No. 3 at the very largest. I have shot geese with No. 8 and with SG, but neither was my choice.[1]

Having chosen the shot size, now for the powder. Black powder I rule out on account of the pillar of fire by night and cloud by day. Smokeless powders are mostly either 33-grain powders or 42-grain powders. With 33-grain powders the standard load for a 3 in gun is 1¼ oz of shot, while with 42-grain powders it is 1½ oz of shot. Therefore a 42-grain powder is best for wildfowling. Amongst these 42-grain powders are Amberite, Shultze, and a new modified Smokeless Diamond. My own preference is for Amberite; I have shot as well with it as with anything else, and I have confidence in it. It does have rather a larger flash than modified

[1] When ordinary 2½ in cartridges are being used for duck shooting, I am convinced that 'fives', 'sixes', or 'sevens' are best. Personally I always use 'sixes' from a game gun. 'Threes' may be used for geese, but anything larger than 'threes' makes too open a pattern.

Smokeless Diamond, so the latter may be better to use at night; but I shot badly and so lost confidence in it and returned to my Amberite.

I find that my cartridges contain a bare one and a half ounces of shot and fifty grains of Amberite powder. The felt wad between powder and shot is seven-sixteenths of an inch thick. These ingredients and the usual card wads completely fill a 3 in cartridge case, so that there is no room for any more shot even if it was wanted. To decrease the powder is not practical and the felt wad is also already as thin as is consistent with its function, so the shot cannot be increased.

The other components of a cartridge are case, wadding, and cap. I always use ' water resisting ' cases. They cost more, but I find them more economical. When I have had non-water resisting cases I have usually had to throw a good many away as they swelled and grew furry or even fell to pieces. Only once have I used cartridges treated with a gunmaker's special waterproofing ; it rained and at the end of the morning flight my pocket contained a plum pudding of papier mâché with shot as the currants.

Anyone who loads his own cartridges or has used a muzzle-loader knows the importance of good wadding. It is mainly the quality of the wadding which makes the difference of price in cartridges. The ordinary British caps give very good results and I can see no reason for using the extra large foreign ones.

Since I wrote the foregoing, a change has occurred. The Alphamax cartridges recently introduced by Imperial Chemical Industries are now (1936) revolutionizing wildfowling ammunition. They are loaded with Neoflak, which is a semi-dense powder. Thirty-five grains of Neoflak occupies only five-sevenths of the space occupied by fifty grains of Amberite. Thus there is more space for shot, without decreasing the wadding. This space takes one and three-quarter ounces of shot, and that charge is well suited to the thirty-five grains of Neoflak.

There is only one disadvantage to this ammunition : the heavy recoil. But in a moderately heavy gun this increase in recoil is not noticed unless a large number of shots are fired ; and how often does anyone have a chance of firing a real lot of shots at geese ?

The cases of these cartridges are coated with cellulose to make them waterproof, and are excellent for all ordinary uses. In a wet pocket they do not grow furry like the usual wet-resisting cases. But in a wet atmosphere they will swell just as easily.

When you have found a kind of cartridge which you like using, stick to it ; the confidence which you put in it is worth almost as much as what the cartridge loader puts into it.

There is no greater waste of time [1] than loading twelve-bore cartridges by hand, when they can be bought. It is never necessary to carry more than three different loads : for knots, ducks, and geese. The people who take out six or seven different loads never have the right one in the gun at the right moment. It is these people who usually load their own cartridges, because they keep a small stock of each kind of load. If only they would leave their AA and SSG at home and let those high geese go on undisturbed they would lose nothing.

Beware of exceptionally cheap foreign cartridges. One winter a friend of mine bought a quantity of very cheap and very waterproof foreign shells. We used them for cripple-stopping when punting, and they were excellent. Many were left unused at the end of the season and they spent the summer with other cartridges in my gunroom. The following September I went out in the punt and again took these foreigners for cripple-stopping. We pursued a crippled shoveller and fired fourteen shots at it at ranges down to fifteen yards, then we killed it with an oar. Some of the cartridges went off like dynamite and

---

[1] If the reader loads his own cases, he can skip this paragraph, as he is sure to be incurable.

scattered the shot far and wide, some were roman candles, and others were fountains of sparks. The English cartridges which had been kept with them were all perfectly good and gave good results at everything from geese to snipe.

With cartridges loaded with different shot it is useful to have them differently marked. Wet resisting cases can only be had in one colour, so, if these are used, they must be marked with ink or very thin paint. A small blob of sealing wax on the top wad can be felt in the dark, and is sometimes useful, until it falls off. Any cartridge can be coated with a thin film of cellulose and is beautifully proof against water, but I have found that they swell in a wet atmosphere.

Many people who go out fowling take shots at the most enormous ranges ; they are aided and abetted in this by the class of gunmaker who leads them to believe that guns of his manufacture are made to kill ducks at a hundred yards. No shoulder gun yet made can consistently kill fowl at one hundred yards and, if it could, it would blow a bird to smithereens at thirty, and even at forty the bird would only be fit for soup. And there are very few people who could hold such a gun straight enough to kill an average of one bird with three shots.

I have already shown that large shot will

not give a killing pattern and small shot, which will give the pattern, has no killing power at long ranges. The whole art of fowling consists of getting the fowl within range. Occasionally a really long shot comes off, and that only tempts the shooter to try it again. If the fowler considers forty yards as the maximum range for shooting at geese and fifty yards for ducks he kills more and disturbs less.[1] If geese are shot at when flighting 200 feet above the ground, thereafter they will increase their altitude. If they are not shot at, they will gradually get slacker until one day they flight well within range. In the season 1928-9 I inspected the feet of fifty-one pink-footed geese which we shot in Norfolk. Two out of every three had old shot wounds in the feet. No wonder the pink-feet of Norfolk are a bit wild!

It is difficult for someone to go to the coast for a short holiday and let fowl fly over undisturbed, when he might get an odd one if he shot at them all. It is still more difficult when he knows that other people shoot at everything within sight. But if he persists in taking shots at excessive distances he may be sure that others will follow suit. If shot can be heard to smack the bird all at once, the bird is probably within range,

---

[1] With an ordinary 2½ in. twelve-bore cartridge, thirty yards is quite far enough for geese, and forty yards for ducks.

but if the shot is heard pattering on the bird, it is most definitely out of range and should not have been shot at. Whether a shot kills or misses it causes the same amount of disturbance.

It is a most unsporting practice to load a gun with a handful of small balls and fire it at ranges up to 300 yards. Little or no skill is required to get within 200 yards of fowl, and bad luck is the only requisite for hitting one of a mass of birds with this lobbing of balls into their midst. The same remarks apply to those detestable ruffians who fire a rifle into the brown of geese and wigeon as they sit far out on the sand.

When shooting from a boat, a four-bore or eight-bore can be most useful. Then, except in the dark, black powder is as good as any other from a single-barrel gun. A four-bore charge is twice the size of a 3 in twelve-bore charge and can be twice as effective against a flock of wigeon on the tide edge. This boat shooting is really a compromise between punting and shoulder-gunning. When firing a gun from a prone position in a boat, it is sometimes very difficult to hold the left hand in the usual place on the fore-end or the barrel. The best way is to rest the barrel on the coaming of the boat, and hold the under-side of the stock with the left hand which should also be almost touching the right cheek. In this way the gun can be held really tight. I have often fired my four-bore like this and have never had any bad kick. I have had, at various times, three most unpleasant kicks; one from a ten-bore which weighed only $7\frac{1}{4}$ lb, one from an eight-bore when I had a stone wall behind my shoulder, and one from my 3 in twelve-bore when lying on my back shooting at a goose straight above me. But with a well-balanced gun held tight to the shoulder, and room for the whole body to give a little, I have never had an unpleasant kick, even from my muzzle-loader of 1 in bore.

A wildfowler may come home with his gun covered in mud, and wet with salt water. First remove the mud and water. An oily rag will not absorb water, so first use old newspaper, then a rag which has no oil on it. An old toothbrush is best for cleaning the sides of the rib and other awkward corners. Avoid driving mud or sand into the mechanism. After cleaning and drying the outside, clean the inside. 3 in cartridges seem to cause more leading than ordinary ones. A stiff bristle brush, or sometimes even a wire brush, must be used to remove this leading. After the first cleaning, remove the dirty oil with a clean rag or piece of tow. Then oil the barrels again with clean oil. Pay special attention to

WAITING FOR THE TIDE

cleaning round the strikers as this part of the gun is next the cap, which is the part of the cartridge which produces the most harmful gases. Another old toothbrush is most useful for administering clean oil to awkward corners. Always keep your ' clean ' cleaning tools separate from your ' dirty ' cleaning tools, and use each for its proper purpose. If your gun has been submerged, through your falling in, or any other cause, the action must be taken down and dried and oiled. A sea of oil is little more protection than a thin film, and catches a lot more dust. Sand and grit often get under the safety catch. Some safety catches may be lifted with a knife blade and so are easily cleaned. Curlews' pin feathers are excellent for cleaning under safety catches. Never use brute force on a gun.

In my gun-case I keep a cleaning rod, wire brush, bristle brush, and slotted jag for use with flannel patches (I have given up using tow). Some flannel patches, a clean oily rag, a dirty oily rag, a clean tooth brush and a dirty tooth brush and a tin of oil, also a piece of old towel for drying off water. Personally I always use Young's ·303 oil because of its anti-nitro fouling properties.

I have a strong dislike for painted gun barrels. The paint may make them less conspicuous, but so does rust without paint. With paint on the barrels it is impossible to see the rust, which is usually there ; consequently the rust is allowed to go on. Varnish is a good protection against salt water, and the rust can be seen through it and dealt with at once.

Chapter II

CLOTHING AND IMPEDIMENTA

As to clothing, everyone has his own fancies. Some writers on fowling tell the fowler exactly what he should wear, beginning at his skin and working outwards. Few, if any, of his readers follow his instructions. But the beginner can save himself some trouble, discomfort, and expense by learning from one who has been taught by experience. Nearly everyone agrees that rubber thigh boots are better than leather ones or fishing waders. Rubber boots are easier to wash, do not need oiling, and have no seams through which to leak. They are lighter than the leather fishermen's boots which are procurable in this country. If they are punctured they can be mended in a few minutes with a motor or cycle tyre patch. My gun case contains a small 'Romac' outfit for this purpose. Boots should be large enough for two pairs of thin socks, but not large enough to get sucked off by deep mud. A heavy 'tread' on the soles prevents slipping, but for boat work it is a nuisance because of the difficulty of cleaning out the mud. The inside of the boots should be carefully dried every day. The best way of doing this is to turn down the tops and stand the boot upright, on its sole, on top of a radiator or hot water tank. If there is neither of these, place the boots with their soles to the fire. The thick soles will stand a great deal of heat, but the thin uppers will not, so be careful not to heat them. Since I have treated my boots in this way they have lasted three times as long as they used to, despite all the doubts of onlookers and boot merchants. Fishing waders have the advantage that the wearer can sit down in water, if he wishes to, or wade across deep creeks : but they are most uncomfortable to walk in. Running in waders is unbearably hot. I once shot thirty-five knots and dunlins with two barrels : I was wearing waders and when I had finished collecting the last cripple I might as well have been in a Turkish bath.

Trousers are more comfortable than breeches, inside long boots. A waistcoat is the better for a flannel back instead of the usual thin one. An ordinary jacket is best for dry land, but a ' golfing jacket ' is better for boat work or mud-larking ; its pockets are not lower than the hips, so do not droop into the mud or water. A thin jacket may be made grass colour on the outside, and sand colour on the inside, and worn inside out when required. Get a shooting coat paler than usual : most people show up darker than the surrounding ground. When a coat is wet it appears darker than when it is dry. The more pockets it has the better.

A cap worn back to front is the nearest approach to ideal. A brim low down over the ears does not help in locating sounds overhead. For a lying pit, a sand coloured beret is best. It has no brim to stick up in front, or, if worn at the back, to act as a trowel for digging up sand and putting it down the back of one's neck. A few black safety pins, in the top of the cap, can be used for adding extra camouflage such as grass or leaves. In wet weather a hat with a brim all round prevents the little trickles down one's neck. In really stormy weather a sou'-wester is the only headgear which will keep out the wet. Its great disadvantage is that its brim, coming well down past the ears, deflects a great deal of sound. A light sou'-wester takes up little space when folded and in a pocket, a beret takes up even less space. In stormy weather both can be taken without any inconvenience. Of course, if one's hair is of a good camouflage colour there is no need for a cap, except as protection against the weather. Fowl do not like the apparition of a black fuzzy wuzzy peering over a creek bank. A pair of mittens or wristlets will help in cold weather. A piece of rabbit skin and an elastic band makes an excellent wristlet.

For shooting in snow, a white Balaclava helmet and a white kennel coat or butcher's coat are excellent. The skirts of the long coat hide boots when kneeling; so the bird merely sees a face and a gun barrel, the stock being hidden by one's forearm. When wearing this outfit I have had geese glide low over my head and settle within thirty yards, though I had practically no cover. And I have had a peregrine falcon screaming with rage at my, apparently, ownerless face which was imitating his own noise.

For stormy weather an oilskin is the best, but it is bulky, and can seldom be bought in a colour which does not contrast with the surrounding landscape. However, a thin coat of paint seems not to be harmful to an oilskin, and any colour scheme that takes one's fancy can be painted on. For intermittent use I have found a light waterproof, costing 10s 6d, to be excellent. See that there is no hiatus between bottom of waterproof and top of thigh boots. Do not have pockets with vertical openings, they always let in water. Horizontal openings can be protected by a flap, which should be twice the size of any ready made pocket flap I have yet seen.

Cartridges are best carried in a belt. It does not slap about when running, or alter its balance when jumping, like a bag does. Different kinds of cartridges can be put in different parts of the belt. Worn under a coat, they keep dry and away from the mud, and their brass ends do not gleam. I prefer a leather belt, with open ends to the cartridge loops. If the loops stretch enough to let the cartridges fall through, bind some strong string round the belt and inside the loop, thereby filling up the surplus space. If a cartridge extractor is tied on to the belt, it will not be left at home when required. A belt which has metal clips may be quicker to load from, but the clips tear the lining of a coat. Personally I seldom load from my belt, merely using it to carry extra cartridges, and loading from my pocket.

A waterproof bag is useful to sit or lie on and to carry dead birds, decoys, waterproof, etc. A 5 ft length of oilskin with eyelets at the sides of two-thirds of its length can be laced together to form a bag 20 inches deep, with a flap of the same depth. If the lacing is undone the whole 5 foot length can be used to lie on. The excuse for carrying the bag is that one wants to sit on it, so one need not be ashamed of bringing it home empty. A net bag is the most handy thing for carrying game. One large enough to carry twenty ducks is, when empty, less than the size of a dead teal. The net is made on a 1 in brass ring at the bottom and has a small brass ring on each mesh at the top. Running through these small rings is a draw string which forms part of the sling. The other end of the sling is attached to the big brass ring at the bottom of the net.

For digging pits in sand or mud, a light, cheap,

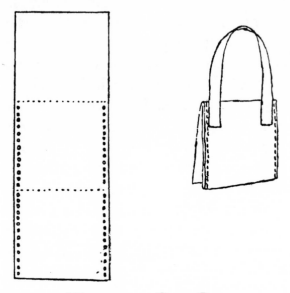

WATERPROOF GAME BAG

kitchen coal shovel, which can be bought for sixpence or ninepence, is quite adequate. It is as well to take a bit of sacking to wrap round the sharp edges of the shovel and so prevent it from cutting the bag. Something for the dog to sit on will not only add to his comfort but will tend to keep him sitting where he was told to.

A rucksack is far the best thing in which to carry a lot of luggage. An ordinary game bag, or the one just described, can instantly be converted into a rucksack by the attachment of a string from the sling to each of the bottom corners, as shown in the sketch.

For punting I wear a waistcoat, because of its pockets being useful, over which I wear one

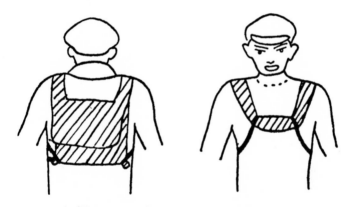

How the Rucksack is Worn

or more sweaters, and over all an anorak. The waistcoat pockets are the ones which keep dry longest and so seem to me the best for watch, matches, etc. The best sweaters are those made by the Faeroe islanders. Their general colour is almost white, unbleached wool spotted with darker colours, so they are most inconspicuous against a background of sea or sky. As this wool contains all its natural grease it is almost waterproof, unlike most English wool which has all the grease removed from it. The anorak is an Eskimo garment which they make from any material : leather, fur, or cloth. The Greenland Eskimo, in summer, wear a cotton anorak.

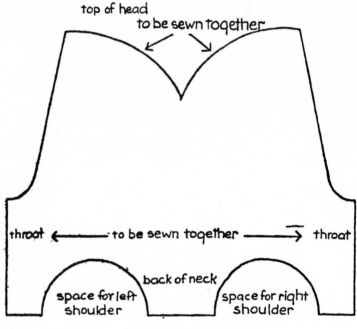

HOOD OF ANORAK

My original anorak was made by a Greenlander at Jakobshavn in West Greenland and the diagram should suffice for anyone who wishes to have a similar one.[1] Closely woven cotton

[1] The diagram shows only the hood : the remainder of the garment being like a tail-less shirt.

is the best material that I have yet used. It is almost windproof, is easily washed, and can be had in any colour. The hood keeps the head and ears warm enough without being unpleasantly hot, prevents water going down the back of the neck, and conceals dark coloured hair. A white one should be used for punting on dull days and a light grey or brown one for bright days. Of course, it can be made double, white on one side and darker on the other, so as to be turned inside out when so required. Pockets can be placed wherever the wearer prefers.

If the weather is not cold, the anorak takes up little space under the side deck. Then, if cold comes on, the anorak serves much the same purpose as the windproof clothing which is worn by Arctic explorers ; keeping in the heat of the body and keeping out the outer air, without becoming sweaty.

When shoulder gunning, too many clothes prevent the gun butt from coming properly to the shoulder. If the outer coat is windproof there is no need for large quantities of sweaters.

A compass is one of the things which should always be taken out by a wildfowler, whether ashore or afloat. But it must be remembered that iron or steel will attract the needle. The steel clips of a cartridge belt are the worst offenders. Once, on Edge Island in the Spitzbergen Arctic,

I spent a long time walking round in circles in a fog. I wished to go due South, and it was some time before I discovered that the centre of my stomach was always due North, whichever way I faced. I had laid down my rifle and sheath knife, but had forgotten the steel of the belt clips.

Field glasses are essential to the punter and almost essential to the shoreshooter. Size and weight do not count for much with the punter, but are all important to the shore shooter. A magnification of about seven diameters is best and a wide field of vision is essential for use in dusk and dawn. Periscopic glasses are the best thing for use in stalking fowl, as the fowler's head then never comes in view of the birds. In a punt they are most useful, for the same reason.

A telescope can be very useful, but when shore shooting it is an extra piece of luggage. When punting, especially when punting from a following boat or yacht, a telescope can be a great asset.

No book on wildfowling would be complete without some mention of decoys. They can be useful in nearly every branch of fowling with a shoulder gun. Those which are sold in shops are nearly all unsuitable for one reason or another. Wooden decoy ducks, as sold, are bulky, heavy, and usually the wrong shape and colour. A decoy duck should be incapable of capsizing. This means that it must be hollow, or else made of some material which is much lighter than wood, and have a lead keel. The head of a decoy duck should be down on its back, not up on the top of a startled looking neck. The shape should be that of a live duck, not the shop produced form of an emaciated dead one.

Inflatable rubber decoys are much too expensive. Nobody wants to expend ten pounds on decoys which are so perishable. If some toy manufacturer would produce a cheap rubber duck, properly coloured, I feel sure that they would sell both as decoys and as children's toys. It must be as easy to make a life-like looking duck as to make a swan or a crocodile. I have used cloth, duck shaped covers containing an inflated penny balloon ; but they are too much trouble to blow up and tie up.

Home made decoys can be made of wood and hollowed out. Their great disadvantage is their bulk. They can be made in such a way that their heads plug in like a cork into a bottle. To carry them, the heads are all put in a bag, and the bodies are threaded on a stick or cord which passes through the holes where the heads go. The lead weights can hook into a screw eye on the under-side.

If decoys are not wanted to float, they are comparatively simple to make. Perhaps the easiest to make are a wire netting framework neatly covered with painted cloth. Their disadvantage is that they easily lose their shape. Wooden ones are probably the best in the long run, though something on the principle of a " Max Baker decoy pigeon " should be quite good.

When painting decoys it is essential that they should not be made shiny. Wooden decoys can be rasped with a very coarse rasp, to make them ' woolly ' before being painted. This keeps them dull, even when wet. Poplar is a good wood for decoys, because it can be cut like cheese, without regard to the direction of the grain. Also, it becomes very ' woolly ' when rasped.

The placing of decoys, so that they will attract fowl in such a way as to offer the best chances to the fowler, can only be learnt by experience. A very common fault is to place all the decoys head to wind. If the decoys are to represent feeding birds they should be placed facing in all directions ; for resting birds they should be facing within ninety degrees of the direction of the wind. Sometimes they should be within a few yards of the fowler ; at other times they are best a long way off, even well out of range. Sometimes one flock, at others two or three scattered parties. Everything depends on the local conditions, strength of wind, and other details. The only way of learning is by individual experience.

Decoy waders should have wire legs. Wooden legs are either too thick or too fragile. Curlew's beaks can be made of stiff rubber tube ; this will not break off, or make holes in a bag.

Portable hides, made of canvas or hessian, are sometimes very effective for curlew flighting or for duck flighting in the dusk. A square sheet can be set up on two sticks and held with guy ropes and cords. A triangular sheet can be held up by one stick in the centre and a peg at each of the bottom corners. The pegs and stick should be placed in such a way that a line drawn from one peg to the stick forms nearly a right angle with a line from the other peg to the stick. An observation hole can be made near the top of the sheet. If there is any natural cover available it is far better to use it than to use an artificial hide.

A barrel sunk in the ground is the best hide of all, if it is large enough. But an ordinary beer barrel is much too small. If the barrel is sunk in waterlogged ground it must be attached to something which will prevent it floating up to the surface. Two crossed beams can be bolted to the bottom, and buried with it. A frame can be made of three or four beams, of such a size that it slips over the top of the barrel but cannot be forced past the bulge at the middle of it. I once saw three people trying to force a barrel down into a hole full of water: it had not occurred to them to fill the barrel with water, and so to sink it. It is only worth putting down a permanent hide like this in a place which is private, or almost so. Attached to the barrel, there must be a bucket on a cord. If the bucket has one or two small holes in it, so much the better; because it will not float out of the barrel and lie on the mud, which it might otherwise do. The small holes are no inconvenience when baling.

For building butts and pulpits any local material can be used. Reeds are the most usual. If portable reed screens are wanted, they are fairly easily woven like this :—Four stakes are set firmly in the ground in a row; the length of the row being less than the required height of the screen. A similar row of four stakes is set up three yards in front of the first row. The tops of both rows of stakes should be about 4 feet from the ground. A string is stretched from each stake of one row to the corresponding stake of the other row. Another four strings each have one end attached to one row of stakes, the other end to a stick which is held in a horizontal position by the 'weaver'. These last strings must be placed parallel to each other, and be of such a length that the weaver's stick comes beyond the second row of stakes. The weaver holds his stick high overhead, while another person puts

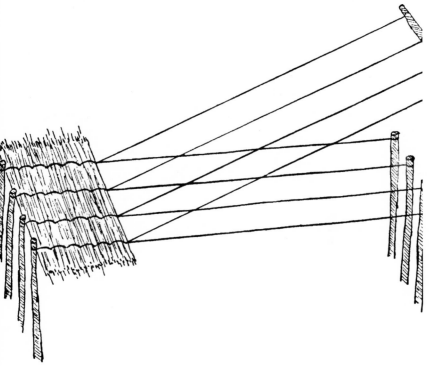

LOOM FOR MAKING REED SCREENS

some reeds between the two sets of strings. The weaver then lowers his stick to near the ground, thereby securing the first lot of reeds. Another bunch of reeds is put between the two strings, of which the fixed one is now the upper.

The weaver raises his stick again, and so secures the second bunch. By repeating these movements, 3 yards of screening is quickly made. Each bunch is put alternately above and below the fixed string. A few short bits of string are tied round the pairs of strings, to secure them together, in case of a breakage, so that only a small bit of screen would fall to bits if a breakage occurred. Then the strings are undone from the stakes and the stick, and reattached so that the weaving is continued. Any length of screening can be made thus.

CHAPTER III

DOGS

To my mind a dog is almost essential to a flight shooter. There are people who say that geese smell a dog although they do not smell human beings : this is so futile as to require no answer. Amongst my flighting companions I have had Labradors, Flat-coated Retrievers, Irish Water Spaniel, Irish Setter, Clumber, Springer, and Norfolk Lurcher, all of which have been helpful. I believe that any breed of dog could be very useful out flighting, and I have seen a nondescript black and tan terrier that was perhaps as good as any—so small that a pocket kept her warm and dry, yet capable of bringing a goose out of the sea and with a good enough nose to find the most obstinate teal on the land.

One often hears the question, " Which is the best dog for wildfowling ? " The only answer that meets with approval is " Yours ". Each breed has its good points and its bad, and individuals of each breed are superb. The old-fashioned Labrador with its double, otter-like coat and tendency to fatness was a grand dog, with its blackness and size as the only disad-

vantages.   The type of leggy Labrador which is
so common these days may be a better dog
for moor and covert, but he lacks the thick
coat and layer of blubber to keep out the cold,
and only too often, at the sight of water, down
goes his tail.   The old-fashioned curly coat
has ceased to exist, he was a stocky dog entirely
unlike the long-legged, long-nosed curly coats
of the present day.   The flat-coat has lost his
lovely forehead and now too often has the face
and brains of a crocodile.

The breeds and species of Spaniels are legion ;
some are good water dogs, others are not.

The conclusion is that individual dogs of any
breed may be as good as individuals of any other,
but one thing to be sure of is that the more
' show blood ' it contains the more it is likely
to be handicapped in its work.

The ideal fowler's dog is obedient, withstands
cold, takes to water and swims well, retrieves
anything, and has a good nose, eyes, and ears
which are each used for their rightful purposes.
It is not too large to go in a car or too small to
carry a goose.   Its coat does not hold water and
its colour is inconspicuous.   In fact it is an
extremely rare animal.

The first law of obedience is to sit where and
when told, and remain sitting until further orders.
Often, on the saltings, the fowler is in a creek full

"LARGE ENOUGH TO CARRY A GOOSE"

of mud and water. It is unfair to the dog to ask
him to sit there too ; he has no waders. The dog
must be placed some distance away, in the nearest
dry cover, or, if there is no cover, placed still
further away in a position where he is likely
to act as a flanker. The most difficult thing to
train the dog to do is, when he has been called
up to retrieve a bird, then, to go back to his
position and lie down again. At first all dogs
interpret the order to go back as meaning that
they are in disgrace ; some never learn otherwise,
and so are apt to sulk and become difficult
to handle.

Really, to sit when told, come into heel when
told, and go back to position when told are all
the tricks required. A dog which does not carry
naturally, is not worth bothering with. If he
has to be taught to carry, sooner or later he
discovers that his master cannot see in the
dark, and then the birds get left lying where
they fall, or worse still, are moved and dropped
again.

If a dog is to withstand cold he must be fit
and healthy. If he can carry a little fat and still
be fit, so much the better, but fitness is a greater
cold resister than fatness. There are two types of
waterproof coats for dogs ; the furry and the
greasy. The Labrador had a close fine fur under-
lying the outer coat of hair. This was almost

waterproof, the dog might look wet but the skin was usually dry. I have seen no other sporting dog with this type of coat so well developed. The greasy coat reaches its climax in the Chesapeake Bay dog. If fingers are wriggled into the thick coat of one of these dogs, they become covered with smelly grease. This grease, which is under all the thick coat, makes these dogs absolutely waterproof. Unfortunately they do not make pleasant house companions owing to their smell. This greasy coat is found in many other breeds of dog, but not to such a marked degree. The old Irish Water Spaniels had it, but many of their modern successors have inherited the non-greasy wool of the poodles which have been used to resurrect the breed. As a result, they have to carry some few extra pounds of water in their coats.

For duck shooting in big broads and mosses a dog cannot well be too large and strong. He may have to spend much of the day hunting through water and then be expected to perform his duties as a retriever. A small dog would be worn out with swimming where a large one has merely been paddling.

Nearly every dog will take to water if it is approached in the right way. Never throw or force it into the water. There are three factors of a dog's character, which can be worked on to break down its fear of water; jealousy, excitement, and fear of losing its master.

If a dog is afraid, avoid letting it go into deep or cold water. When weather and water are both warm is the time for training. Jealousy of another dog is the best method. A shallow ford, or cattle drinking place in a pond is as good a place as anywhere. A dummy, or dead bird, is thrown in ; first in the very edge of the water where the pupil need barely wet his paws, then gradually further and further until he is swimming. Each time he refuses or delays, another dog is sent to grab it from under his very nose. He sees the other dog made a fuss of and his jealousy soon gets the better of him. If this fails one can ford a stream and hope he will follow; again starting with an inch or two of water and gradually choosing deeper places. One or two attempts, of either method, in a day are plenty. If the dog gets too much of anything he will be sickened of it.

Unless he is very chicken-hearted he will succumb to the excitement of moorhen hunting, but as moorhens are a vice this must be regarded as the last contingency. But whatever method is used it must be remembered that the water cannot be too warm, or too shallow for a start, or the training be too gradual.

When a dog takes willingly to the water, train him to hunt well out on the far bank, on the far side of an island, and on the far side and in the heart of a reed bed. Most people throw a dummy into the water where it is visible to the dog, and never progress further with their water training. There are few things more annoying than to be able to see a bird lying dead fifty yards beyond the far bank of the river, and to be unable to get the dog out and away from the water's edge. Some dogs never seem to realize that scent is carried on water as well as air, when there is an upstream wind and the dog strikes a water-born scent it often turns down stream in the wrong direction. Good swimmers usually hold their noses closer to the surface and so make the right discovery sooner. Some dogs will actually dive under water; I have never seen one myself, but I had a Clumber Spaniel which would put her head under to look for a wounded duck which dived. She was an excellent swimmer and would sometimes swim over a diving duck with her head submerged and her eye on the duck, so that when at length it had to come up for air, there was her mouth all ready to receive it.

Another Spaniel, a Springer, which I have now was sent by me to get some moorhen's egg from a nest in a pond. She brought out two at once, and I dropped one of them in the water. She saw me feeling for it and realized what had happened, so put her head under the surface

and blew bubbles, presumably trying to wind it !
This happened only last week (April, 1936).

I had one dog who would never learn that
it was hopeless trying to swim against a current,
and she would always turn her head upstream
and fight against it. Once she was nearly drowned
because she fought against the stream for so
long that she was carried down into a place
where both sides of the river were frozen over
with thick ice. Fortunately there was a long
fence rail lying loose on the bank, and I was able
to break open a canal for her. Never send a dog
on to ice that may not bear. If it falls through
it will be lucky if it climbs out again. As Colonel
Peter Hawker says : " A bitch is always to be
preferred to a dog in frosty weather, from being,
by nature, less obstructed in landing on the ice."
In the same paragraph of his famous book,
*Instructions to Young Sportsmen in all that relates
to Guns and Shooting*, he makes another great
statement, " For a punt, or canoe, always make
choice of the smallest Newfoundland dog that
you can procure ; as the smaller he is, the less
water he brings into your boat after being sent
out. . . ."

The best boating dog I ever had was a small
Springer Spaniel. She is the only dog that I have
ever taken out punting with a big gun. Pansy
was her name. She used to accompany us on

the days when a spring tide was high after dusk, because on those days we would often get a shot at wigeon, or geese, right up amongst the tussocks of the saltings. Then Pansy was invaluable for catching cripples as well as dead birds. She could always be trusted to do what she was told, and so used to be kept dry and warm until this last moment of the day. Her place was alongside the gunner, and there she would lie, shaking with excitement and knowing that she was not allowed to put up her head. Her nose would be quivering with suppressed excitement as the punt came upwind to a flock of fowl, but never a move or a sound would she make. Then, at the roar of the big gun, she would jump on to the fore deck and stand on the bows waiting for some dead bird to pass within reach, or for the punt to run ashore, or for an order to go overboard.

When flighting on shore, she would not even glance at any passing bird other than ducks and geese; and these she usually spotted before I did, thereby being of the greatest assistance in warning me of their approach. If a goose was hard hit and sloping away in the dark, she would follow in the direction it had gone and, on reaching it, bite its neck and then return for me and lead me to it. She was an adept at marking fallen birds both by sight and sound. She had

as varied a career as any dog, having proved useful
in all branches of shooting, hare, rabbit, and rat
catching, deer shooting and fox hunting (Highland style).   Otters were her pet aversion, in
fact, if she came on the track of an otter, while
duck shooting, she was useless for most of the
rest of the day, as she thought of nothing and
looked for nothing except the otter.   Perhaps it
was the glamour of the unknown, for I doubt
if she ever saw one.   Then, one day, she found
one in an osier holt in the flooded Cambridgeshire washes when all the water was frost bound
and people were skating everywhere.   An otter
does not move fast over ice so she soon came
up with it, her long sought quarry, and grabbed
it ignominiously by its rudder.   Then she had
a great shock at being severely bitten and would
not close with it again.   Unfortunately the otter
took to a railway embankment and was killed
in trying to pass under the middle of a train.
I thought the end of Pansy had come, for she
was almost uncontrollably excited, but the
shrieked command had its effect and she dropped
in her tracks within two yards of the whirling
wheels, the remains of the otter still moving
about just in front of her.   Had she been any
less obedient she would have gone on and met
her death beside her quarry.

A wildfowler's dog can have a very hard time

in really cold weather, and it is up to his master to minimize his discomfort. The first consideration is general health and fitness. A clean, healthy coat keeps a dog far warmer than a dirty one which is twice as thick. A 'staring' coat is not a bit waterproof. As I have said before, good condition is the best aid against cold.

People argue about the rival merits of keeping a dog in the house and in a kennel. A house dog learns far more about his master's ways and need not be one whit the softer. But a bumptious dog may be ruined by living in the house, finding that he can get his own way with the other members of the household and so ceasing to pay due respect to his master. Such dogs are the exception, except in households which are hopelessly soft and sloppy about dogs.

An outside kennel should be shady in summer and catch the sun in the winter. Its sleeping place should be absolutely free from draught. On no account should any dog be allowed to sleep on a stone or concrete floor. If the sleeping place has such a floor a wooden bench is essential. Whatever the floor is made of, a bench is an asset, as there are always draughts on every floor. Good clean wheat straw is the best bedding. Wood shavings get mixed up in the dog's coat and sometimes cause irritation, while wood chips are not warm enough in winter.

There always has been and always will be much controversy about dog shows and field trials. Only one dog in each class can get the first prize and so there must be some disappointed owners. But some judges get a bee in their bonnet about certain points and so overlook other points which are far more important, and the prize goes to a dog which has that one point exaggerated. Then the dog is used for stud purposes because the puppies of a winner are more saleable than those of an unknown dog. And that is one way in which the rot starts.

Then at field trials it is impossible to give each dog exactly the same work. Every effort is made to produce the same sort of work for each dog, but it obviously cannot be exactly the same. Then the judge does not know all the dogs. If he suspects a certain habit, then he can try to prove it, but if he does not suspect it he may not find out.

One day a friend and I were shooting together. I shot a cock pheasant which fell, apparently dead, in a thick reed bed. A young dog was sent for the bird. We heard the dog going about in the reeds, stopping and going on and stopping again. Eventually the dog came out with nothing. Then my dog was put in and came out with nothing. Then we went in and I found the feathers where the bird had fallen, and a few feathers in other places. The dog's owner said the bird had run but I thought otherwise. My old dog was trained not to touch a bird that had once been picked up and as it was a good scenting day and my dog displayed no interest and owned to no line I felt sure that the first young dog had moved the bird and then left it. A few days later this dog did very well at a big field trial which was held on fairly open country. It was in sight of its handler and so brought everything well to hand. Shortly afterwards the dog was again out shooting with me and again lost a bird in thick cover. Later on two pheasant corpses were found at the places where these two birds were lost.

Now the judge at the field trial could not have discovered this vice in the dog, because there were no reed beds on the ground where the trial was run. That ground had a lot of different types of country in it, but none were impenetrable to the human eye. It would be quite impossible to give each dog every known type of country, and to attempt to do too much in this way leads to entirely artificial staging of the trial.

Water tests are often criticized, sometimes rightly so, for being artificial. Where a sufficiency of game can be driven over water all is well, but where this is not possible the water tests should only be given to the leading dogs and at the end of the day.

Recently there was much criticism in one sporting paper from a writer who said that it was 'unfair' to a dog to ask it to cross water to look for a bird which it had not seen fall. Presumably this man either lived in a waterless country or left many birds to rot on the ground. Many times in each season I find it necessary to send dogs into cover on the far side of water either to retrieve something or to drive something out. Often, on a river, I have known that a wounded duck has gone upstream or downstream, but have not known which bank it has gone to. I keep quiet for long enough to allow it to go ashore, then I go after it with a dog working each bank. If a wounded duck is not chased it will nearly always go ashore. But if it is chased it will keep to the water and keep on diving. Of course if the dog can be put after the bird directly it is wounded then it is often possible to get another shot and finish it off.

When flighting in the cold winter months, I am convinced that it pays to keep the dogs dry for as long as possible, preferably to keep them dry until the end of the flight. Then they are called in and do their work all in one go and are finished with it. Whereas if the dog is sent straight in after the first duck, he gets wet and is then expected to sit still, when of course he gets thoroughly cold. Then either he will not work, or, if he does carry on till the end of the shooting, he does not last many seasons before becoming an old cripple. Never work a dog with a collar on in water. Personally I hate having a collar on any dog while it is working, but in water it can be a real danger. One of my dogs once got hung up by a branch through its collar, and if left to itself would have been drowned. No person could reach the dog because of the soft mud under the water. Mercifully I was able to get within such a short distance that I could shoot through the offending branch and so release the dog. Should a similar accident happen in a really inaccessible place it might well cause the death of the dog.

CHAPTER IV

SHORE SHOOTING

Where ducks spend the day on the sea or on the tidal muds and sands, the shore shooter can only get at them when they are flighting to or from their feeding grounds, or when a high tide moves them within range of some point of the shore. Nearly all successful plans for circumventing these ducks depend, not on getting near to the ducks, but on getting into some position within range of which the duck will come. The novice is often tempted to try and walk up birds on the saltings, because he gets tired of sitting and waiting. If he is content with shooting redshanks, he may get a few shots, but he will get near little that is more worthy, on an open expanse of flat salting.

For a successful plan, all factors which affect the duck must be considered. The expert fowler should be capable of thinking like a duck thinks, in fact he should almost be a duck. A knowledge of the times of rising and setting of sun and moon, of times and heights of tides, of directions and strengths of winds are all essential. Then it is an enormous help to be able to visualize a map of the land and sea with the different feeding grounds and resting places marked on it. The flight lines of duck change as the feeding grounds change : in September the duck may go to the barley stubbles, in November to the potato fields, and in hard frosts to anywhere where there is unfrozen water. The position which is best for getting the duck in September may be quite hopeless later on in the season.

Then the strength and direction of the wind may control where the ducks rest on the estuary. There is a bay where I have shot many wigeon. The west side of this bay is flat, low lying salting covered with grass like a lawn, the east side is steep and rocky. The extent of the grass is so great that the wigeon, under normal conditions, may flight in at any place on its whole length. But, if there is a strong wind blowing into the bay, the sea becomes rough, and the wigeon all go for shelter in one small river. Then, at flight time, as they are all concentrated in one place, they all flight on one line.

There are many flight shooters who go to some place where they know that duck pass over but do not know why they pass over it. Then the time comes when the duck no longer do pass over it, but the fowler continues going there. Because he no longer sees the duck he says that they have been exterminated or driven

away, and gives as a reason : aeroplanes, punters,
shipping, or some one or other of his particular
bètes noirès. In actual fact, did he but know it,
some geographical feature has changed ;   the
river has gone into a new channel through the
sand or a farm has been laid down to grass or
another farm has been drained. The duck rest
on the channel edge and feed on the arable
ground or the marshes. They cannot be expected
to rest on a waterless sand and feed on dry
grass land, simply because these were the resting
and feeding places of their ancestors. Yet these
fowlers seem to expect to shoot fowl in the
places where they, or their ancestors, did so in
the past.

It is always as well to find out why duck use
a flight line. A slight knowledge of the country
and a look at the map will often show the reason.
Then, if that flight line ceases to be used, the
reason is not so far to seek. A look at the country
and a comparison with its former state shows
the factor which has changed and so enables
the fowler to change his own plans.

This example will make clear my meaning.
On an estuary where I had been flighting for
some years, my best flight line suddenly became
disused. I did not know the seaward estuary,
but I did know the landward farms, and I knew
that the duck had always gone in the direction

of a small lake. An evening spent on the road near the lake showed that the duck were still coming there, but coming from a new direction. A few minutes with the map showed that this direction was from the other side of the estuary. And a conversation with a fisherman showed that there had been a storm which had washed out a sand bar and so formed a lagoon which held water at low tide on this side of the estuary. All the duck had forsaken the channel and gone to this lagoon to rest and wash. By moving my position about a mile I was able once more to get under the flighting ducks.

If the flight shooter is also a punt gunner, or has some other pursuit which takes him on to the estuary, then he sees the changes taking place and is enabled to make great use of this knowledge. I owe many a successful evening and morning to the discovery of new cockle beds, mussel scaups, and weed beds, or to finding that old ones had been destroyed by storms.

When wigeon are coming to feed on a weed bank on the tidal mud, there are two alternatives open to the fowler. Either he can find a suitable position, in which to wait, which lies on the line of the birds as they flight in to their feed; or he can take up his position actually on the feeding place. But, if he chooses the latter, and wishes to be able to go on having sport in the same place in the future, he must leave before the end of each flight. By so doing he allows the last birds to come in undisturbed, and so they return again and soon attract the frightened ones back. If he wishes to leave them completely undisturbed on their feeding ground, which is really the best thing, he can find a suitable scaup, scaur, or rock on the flight line on which to sit and wait their passing by. Or he can sink a barrel or watertight box if he requires more cover. The great advantage of having such a barrel is that the shots can be taken from a standing position and without feet stuck in the mud.

I do not consider it worth while sinking barrels unless I have the place to myself and am able to pick and choose my shooting nights. For most occasions, the dark background of stones or mussel shells is sufficient to break up the outline of a sitting or kneeling man and so conceal him from the fowl. The tide washes out footprints and removes empty cartridge cases and so nothing is left to disclose the position to rival fowlers. So many people, who do not understand wildfowling, consider secrecy to be pure selfishness. To a certain extent it is; but it is perfectly true that if a place is overshot it is soon spoiled, and if it becomes known to more than a select few it is certain to be overshot. The only protection against overshooting is extreme secrecy.

In America, where the vast majority of the land is no more private than the English foreshore and anyone can shoot almost anywhere, provided he has a licence, there are practically no sanctuaries for the wildfowl. They are harassed every day of the open season, and this is one of the great factors in the diminution of American wildfowl. The private estates and farms in this country provide the most perfect sanctuaries for fowl. All the season, with the exception of a very few shooting days, everything is done which can be done, to benefit the fowl. They get their food, water, and shelter, and all their enemies are persecuted. The birds which are shot on the few shooting days form a small proportion of the fowl which inhabit these places. If the same ground was not strictly preserved there would be many fewer birds there and many fewer would be shot; but those which were shot would form a much greater proportion of the birds then living on the place.

Last season (1935–6) was a very bad wildfowling season in certain districts. Various sporting papers published letters from wildfowlers who blamed every conceivable thing for their lack of sport. Amongst the writers were some who blamed the larger duck shoots in the country, saying that they destroyed enormous

quantities of duck. It is my firm belief that these
large duck shoots are the very best sanctuary
that wildfowl can have. The owner has, in his
duck preserve, an asset of great value. He may
either shoot it himself or let it for a sum of
money. That sum of money is directly controlled
by the number of duck which can be shot on
the ground. If the duck population decreases,
then the number that can be shot also decreases,
and so the value decreases. What sane man
would deliberately reduce the value of his own
property? On the contrary, he would try to
enhance the value of it by increasing the number
of ducks.

If that same shooting ground was made as
open to the public as is the foreshore, it would
no longer be a sanctuary. Everyone would shoot
on it and no one would preserve on it. No one
would abstain from shooting for certain periods,
because he would know that someone else would
shoot it even if he did not. In theory that is a
very poor excuse; but theory and human nature
are two entirely different things.

The duck would be driven away from the
ground by disturbance and shortage of food.
Either they would go elsewhere on public
ground and meet with the same treatment or
they would go to some other preserve. In the
latter instance they would be properly looked

after and a good majority would live to reproduce their species. And some of them would serve to keep up the numbers on the overshot public ground.

However, not all ground can be overshot by the shore shooter. Where birds rest far out on the sand, and feed inland, the shore shooter can only shoot at them on flight. If he shoots too much he merely makes the birds fly high out of range; he does not reduce their numbers or drive them away. But, with bernacle geese on some of the Scottish Firths it is a very different story. These birds always feed on the salting and thus their feeding ground is always liable to be disturbed by shore shooters. They must feed every day, and consequently they must be in grave danger every day. Each fowler says the same thing: " If I don't shoot them someone else will, so I might as well do it myself." The result is that the bernacle geese are decreasing very rapidly.

Where a punter or shore shooter is the only one in the district, he preserves his ground in the same way as an owner of a private place. He does not overshoot it or disturb the same ground too often, because he knows that that would spoil his ground for the future. But where there is more than one punter the ground is liable to be overshot. The reason is the same one: " If I don't he will."

It is much the best for each fowler to preserve his own ground with the strictest secrecy. Even then it will be discovered by someone who will let the cat out of the bag. Then the place will be overshot and ruined for some years. After everyone knows that the place is ruined, it may become deserted by fowlers and so again become good for fowl.

There are few places where a flight shooter can hope for more than ten ducks to his own gun on 'free' shooting. I have only exceeded ten on one or two occasions. Once, when we were punting, I walked on to a salting to look down the channel with my field glasses. On the salting I found a fair-sized pool of shallow water, caused by the blocking of a gutter. The pool was fresh rain water and could not have been there more than three days. One glance showed that a great many wigeon had been there the previous night.

We came in early from punting, had a combined lunch and tea, and then I set off for the pool. I took a coal shovel with me and so trimmed up the gutter to afford some concealment. However, the birds did not come till late, when it was dark enough to enable me to take up a position in the open. The early ones were easy to see, but when the late ones came it was too dark for good shooting. This pool was the only shallow fresh water for miles, and it was full of short, sweet grass, so it was an ideal feeding place.   The wigeon realized this and came streaming in ;   singly and in pairs and flocks. If there had been a good sky and if I had shot straighter I might have made a very big bag. However, there are as many ' ifs ' in wildfowling as there are in fishing :   the sky was dark and I did not shoot well.   When it became too dark to see I went home with fourteen wigeon, which is as many as I have ever shot on a single evening flight on the foreshore.

Not far from this spot is a small sandy bay where I have had good sport with mallards at morning flight.   Down the middle of the bay, at low water, there flows a small stream.   In half a dozen places there are rocks at the side of the stream ;   and it is on these rocks that the mallards often sit.   Three of us went there one morning.   We chose a day when the tide was low at dawn, so that we should be able to sit on the rocks.   Each of us chose a different patch of rocks, and there built a small butt of stones and   seaweed.   The mallards flighted straight down the stream, while curlews flew across from the open sand.   One of us was very unfortunate in choosing a patch of rocks which the birds seemed to avoid ;   there was no visible reason why those rocks should have been any worse than the others, it just happened that they were. If the mallards passed at all high or wide of one gun, he would let them go on in the hopes of their going closer to the next gun. In the hour of shooting we got seven mallards, four curlew, and a golden plover. Not a great bag, but a most enjoyable morning. The weather was beautiful and warm, the month being September; and it was a joy merely to be out on the shore on such a day, whether the bag was empty or not. Later on, when the wigeon arrive, there are many of them at this place, but then we prefer to leave the lower part of the bay undisturbed, for the benefit of the punt. However, the shores of the upper part form a good flighting ground.

Here the flat sands are bounded by sand dunes covered with marram grass, and by small patches of grassy salting where there are a few gorse bushes. Perfect hiding places can be found both amongst the marram and the gorse. When I first knew this place there was only one other person who flighted there, and so the birds flew over within easy range. There were mallard, wigeon, and teal, golden plover and curlew, besides grey geese. There was one place in the edge of the dunes, which was like a sunk grouse butt. There was room to stand up in it and still remain concealed from all sides. It was the most perfect flighting place that could be imagined, and was right in the centre of the curlews' flight line; while both ducks and geese also flew over it.

One evening, with the wind blowing off the sea, I sat there waiting for the flight. The sand was dry and the butt was well sheltered, so it was a very comfortable place. Curlews and oyster-catchers were calling out on the sand, and yet more curlews in the fields behind the dunes. Three mergansers were fishing in the stream. The first birds to flight, excepting the gulls, were the curlews which came out from the fields to sleep on the sands. First they came at long intervals behind each other, and then later in companies and battalions. They came low against the wind, passing straight over and to both sides. At one time I had seven birds with seven cartridges as quickly as I could load, and my gun barrels were hot: a rare thing in wildfowling. The curlew flight was tailing off when I heard the geese coming. Their main army flew over the edge of the dunes some half-mile away from my position, but five birds came later and just within range. I heard my first shot hit, and, at the second, the bird set its wings and glided down to the sand where it lay dead with outstretched wings.

A few more curlews came, and I shot one

unfortunate oyster-catcher in mistake for a curlew.
Then the duck started flighting, but the wind
was in their tails and they mostly came too high,
so I only got one mallard and a teal. It had
been a good evening, thoroughly enjoyed by
my dog as well as by myself.

Wigeon shooting at night, on their feeding
grounds, can be great sport. If the best is to
be made of it, the right night must be carefully
chosen; when tide and moon are at their most
suitable phase.

Many wigeon feed on the grass of a large
salting which I know well. They flight in so
late in the evening that the light of the sunset
has all gone, and so they cannot be seen except
by moonlight. With a good moonlight, and
high tides, I have had some good evenings with
them.

One such evening two of us went out on the
salting. The last high tide, driven up by the
wind, had covered the salting and so had left
many pools of water. At the sunset flight a
few mallards came in to these pools, and we
got three between the two of us. Most of the
mallards flew too high, and passed over to the
cultivated land. Then it got too dark for us to
see to shoot anything smaller than a goose.

Out on the mud there was the noise of the
curlews being moved by the tide. Dunlins and

grey plovers were calling as they flew up to the saltings. As the moon rose above the low dark clouds, the grey geese began calling from out on the water. The sky was a perfect background, small, fleecy clouds over it all, except just round the extreme horizon where the clouds were darker. A few curlews and wigeon flew by, but not within range.

When the tide reached the salting's edge, fowl of many species began flighting. They came along the tide edge from east to west, so that we could see them beautifully against the brightest part of the sky. Most of them were just too far out over the water, but some were even on the inland side of us. The tide rose fast, compelling us to move back the whole time. To be too far behind the tide edge meant that the birds would all be out of range; while to be too far on the seaward side meant that the creek banks would be covered and a wetting would be inevitable. As the tide covered each successive point or bank, it flooded the birds off it. If the bank was close to us the birds would come in a disorderly mob; sometimes the curlew were in a veritable cloud. If the bank was far from us the birds had had time to get into formations, and so came over in V's or skeins.

As a bird fell the dog was sent after it immediately. The higher tufts of seablite, standing out of the water, looked just like dead birds, making it difficult for us to pick our birds ourselves. If we were delayed in finding a bird, the tide edge got too far inland, and we had to hurry carefully after it. More haste meant less speed because it meant falling in. Both of us knew this salting intimately. It would have been impossible for a stranger to have got back with dry clothes.

Occasionally we would shoot ducks, and, when the dog brought them, find they were only useless shellducks. The light was not good enough for us to be able to differentiate between the species of duck. Only by their noises could we be certain.

The tide came in so fast that at times we had to run back from it; because, not only did we have to retreat from the tide, but also we had to go a mile along the salting, owing to the geography of the creeks. Five minutes after we had reached the sea wall the whole salting was under water.

Once, some years previously, I had followed up the wrong creek, and been cut off by the tide. I was wearing fishing waders up to my waist, so decided to stand on the highest point and wait for the tide to drop. I tried to make the dog swim to the bank, but it was too far and she would not leave me. Standing still with the tide rising higher and higher, and a wet dog shivering on my shoulders, became rather a cold occupation. Eventually I was so cold that I made for the shore and got wet from head to foot. On the landward side of the sea wall was a lot of very long, coarse grass and some small bushes. From these I managed to make a fire, and took off all my clothes and warmed myself again. It was lucky that I had had a waterproof match container.

That salting has given me some of the best days, as well as nights, with a shoulder gun. One morning flight, in early November, will always remain in my memory.

The moon had already set before we left the car, and the stars were hidden by the thin clouds. The night was so dark that, after leaving the lights of the motor, it was difficult to keep to the path. On one side was the knee-deep mud of the cart track, on the other a deep ditch. The wind was cold enough to make me thankful for my extra waistcoat.

For some way the path went along one side of a potato field ; the long grave making a skyline very close to us. Mallards were quacking as they finished their meal of rotten potatoes. Already some of them were passing overhead to the sea. A dark shape loomed up in front of us : straw stacks and a bullock yard. There was a rustling of straw and loud snortings as the bullocks got the wind of Pansy who was hunting a rat. The rat escaped into the ditch with a splash.

After another two hundred yards we were amongst the long grass on the sea wall. Behind us were the many points of light where the farms and cottages were beginning to awake. In front, in a single line, some of them disappearing and reappearing, were the lights of the channel buoys. The tide was a long way from us, its noise only reaching us faintly. Mallards were beginning to flight in earnest, but it was too dark to see them. There was a pale greenish light in the east, which made us hurry.

The long grass was covered with hoar frost; and Pansy's back was white with the crystals. We tried to avoid filling our long boots with them. R. and I left the bank while P. went on along it. We followed a track which was made by the farm carts as they go out across the salting to fetch sand from the tidal banks. Some way down the track R. went away to the right, to reach his chosen creek, while I went on a bit further.

By then the sky was of a greenish blue, except in the east where it was already beginning to glow with streaks of pink and silver. The outlines of the creeks and the tussocks of seablite were showing indistinctly. It was light enough to see to shoot. A bunch of wigeon whistled past, but I was not quick enough. Fifty yards further on, a noise of approaching geese made me jump into the creek beside which I had been walking. At a hiss, Pansy lay down, hidden amongst the tussocks. The clamour came closer, then circled away and out to sea again.

I climbed out of my hiding place and hurriedly pulled up two or three large clumps of seablite and got into the deepest and narrowest creek I could find. I arranged the clumps round me as extra cover, while Pansy curled up in a growing tussock which I rearranged to hide her.

Now, sitting on my bag, I had leisure to notice things. The glow in the east was turning to a golden brightness while the stars were fading out. Dunlins and grey plovers were darting about with their high pitched piping calls. The last of the mallard were rustling high overhead. Suddenly, a large bird appeared from nowhere, swerved up and back, and was gone. My gun was almost at my shoulder before I realized that it was a short-eared owl.

A whistling from inland made me turn to await a bunch of wigeon ; but they came too high.

Another long spell of waiting was broken by a hoarse grunt from the direction of the sea ;

a thin, wavering line was heading straight for
me. They were geese, and now their clamour was
continuous. They swerved away to the right,
then turned and headed for me again. " Lie
down ! " as Pansy poked her head up. Now
they were within two hundred yards ; Pansy
was hidden again, and I was watching through
the seablite twigs. Now they were fifty yards ;
my gun came slowly to my shoulder, and my
back slowly straightened. At the first shot the
bird next the leader crumpled, and the rest of
the flock flared upwards. The second shot was
fired too hurriedly, and went yards underneath
the shying birds. Pansy was sitting up, looking
in the direction where the goose had landed
with a heavy bump. She was shaking with
excitement and wanting to be off. As I reloaded
I looked to see that no more birds were coming.
A word to Pansy and she was gone. I climbed
out of the creek and went after her. She was
nosing the bird ; a sleek heap of delicate greys
and browns lying amongst the soft lavender-
coloured seablite. A pink-footed goose is a
beautiful bird.

On returning to the creek the goose was
hidden with the field-glasses under some ' crab-
grass ', Pansy went back to her nest and all
was quiet once more.

A continuous stream of gulls was passing

along the shore, from west to east. Redshanks
were beginning to search the creeks for their
breakfast. A few curlew were coming in to the
edge of the saltings. The eastern sky was a glory
of gold while even the west was tinted with rose.
It was a very clear morning; the trees on the
far side of the bay showed clear cut against
the sky, while all nearer objects were clearly
defined.

Two shots sounded from the eastward;
somewhere near where P. should have been.
The distance was too far for me to be able to
see what the shots were fired at.

Another distant clamour of geese was approaching from far out on the mud. Soon I could see
a large skein heading in on the same line as the
first. When they were half a mile away they
veered off to the right, and I saw that another
small bunch was following them. They looked
as though they might be going over R., but no
shot greeted them. Suddenly, the second bunch
flared upwards, and then the sound of two shots
reached me. I had already seen that no birds
were coming my way. In an instant my glasses
were out of their case, and I was watching the
geese. One bird lagged behind the others.
It turned back towards the sea. I jumped
out of the creek and stood up to get a
better view. It set its wings, and I knew it

would not go far. It was down; in a line between the fourth and fifth posts of that flight net.

R. walked out and searched for it but could not find it. I was on the point of taking Pansy over to help him, when he found it. I looked back to seawards in the nick of time. Three hundred yards away was a single goose, heading straight for me.

He came past fifty yards to my left, and I shot him. As he hit the muddy bank of the big creek I saw that he was only winged. While Pansy went straight for him, I ran to lower down the creek. After much splashing, Pansy appeared on top of the bank with the goose. While we were having this cripple chase, seven geese came up unobserved. Had I been hidden they would have come over me.

Two or three skeins of geese were on the move by now, but all were passing too far to the west. A single shot sounded from P's direction, and I could see him walking about looking for something. The tide was running up my creek and was over my ankles. The nearest part of the tide line was about five hundred yards away. There were not many birds on it yet, as some bars further out were still uncovered. I knew that the main lot of geese had not yet come in, and expected them at any

moment.   Curlews and godwits were already
being driven in.

A peregrine passed along the salting's edge.
The rim of the sun was showing, and half the
sky was bare of clouds.   My thoughts were
interrupted by a mighty clamour as a thousand
geese rose from nearly a mile out to sea.   They
were an irregular gaggle at first, but soon they
sorted themselves out into skeins.   They were
going to come in on a frontage of a quarter of
a mile, and appeared to be going to pass all
round me.   Pansy's head was up again :   " Lie
down !   will you never learn to keep your face
down."   They came straight over me, but they
were too high.   Some of them also passed over
R.   They were a grand sight, as they passed
inland with the sun rising under them.

The tide line in front of me was covered with
birds ;   curlew, knots, and dunlin, with a few
godwits, and grey and golden plover.   The flocks
of knots and dunlins performed miracles.   One
moment a flock was white, then black, then golden.
One moment it was a cube, then a pyramid, then
a spiral.   The water was over my knees by now,
and R. was already retreating.   A glance at my
watch showed that the tide still had twenty
minutes to run.   A curlew came past, but just
too far.   Another, following him, came within
range.   I missed him with the first barrel, and

did not fire with the second, as I thought that another curlew was going to offer a better chance. That one fell almost on top of me.

These shots frightened away all the birds from my vicinity; but, in a minute, more birds began to come. The tide was nearly over my long boots, and I was on the point of getting out of the creek, when a big flock of curlew came. Automatically, I crouched down; and, of course, the water did come over the top. But I got one of the curlews.

Both of the others were firing a few shots. A pair of wigeon came past, offering a long shot which I missed. Then I had to get out of my creek and lie flat on my back; whereupon, a small bunch of geese came along the shore and saw me.

Then a flock of knots came so low that they were past me before I saw them. I imagined that I felt the wind of their wings, so close did they pass. With my two barrels I got seven of them. Without a dog they would have been difficult to find amongst the seablite.

When the tide ebbed, the countless waders moved further out on to the mud. Each moment their ranks became more scattered. It was no use waiting any longer, so I started back to the sea wall. The wind had dropped right away, and the sun was very warm. The salting was glittering with the melting hoar frost. Hoodie crows and gulls were scavenging about. A hare slipped away in front of me. Three black tramp steamers were coming down the channel, and behind them a shrimper with gunning punt in tow.

On reaching the bank, I found that the other two were already there, lying basking in the sun. R. had got another pinkfoot and two curlew, while P. had two wigeon and three knots. We were all delighted with the morning, which had been a really good one.

This salting, and the mud beyond it, could always provide us with some kind of sport. If times and tides were not suitable for our getting at the geese, there were the ducks. If ducks failed, there were always the waders. We used not to worry about the dunlins and redshanks and other small waders, which are of little use when they have been shot. Curlews, knots, godwits, and grey and golden plovers were the only waders which we tried to shoot. Once I missed a bird which was about the size of a redshank, had yellow legs and a strange call. Three days later a yellowshank, a straggler from America, was killed further down the coast. I often wonder if it was the bird which I missed. Other rare birds would often be seen on this salting. Greenshank and spotted redshank, whose calls revived my memory; making the mud and salting fade away to be replaced, for an instant, by the wide, open bogs and dark spruce forests of Lapland where these birds breed.

Once P. and I were sitting on our punt far out on the sand, waiting for the tide to flow. We were eating our lunch of sandwiches. Running about on the sand, close to us, was a single sanderling. I told P. how a sanderling used to come to my camp in Spitzbergen and eat the scraps which we threw out. He thought I was joking ; so I threw some meat from my sandwich towards the little bird. The sanderling soon found it and began pecking it and shaking it just as the Spitzbergen bird had done with our bacon rind. I must admit that I had not really expected this one to eat our food.

Peregrine falcons and hen harriers were neither of them uncommon, while short-eared owls were often very plentiful. One morning we found the whole salting full of sparrowhawks. They must have immigrated during the night. Just before sunrise there were hawks rushing about in all directions, and the dunlins had a poor time. I have never, either before or since, seen so many hawks at once.

Fortunately, the days when wildfowlers shot everything, including hawks and grebes, are gone. No longer does the puntsman consider himself badly dressed without his grebe skin cap. The professional wildfowler no longer has a market for the big hawks. The indiscriminate collecting of birds serves no purpose and should not be done. The discriminating, scientific collector does serve a purpose.

The wildfowler often shoots uncommon ducks, and therefore I think it is a good thing for any fowler to make a small collection of the true wildfowl. But let it stop there. Begin with the geese and end with the diving ducks. If a fowler definitely goes out to slaughter a spoonbill or an osprey, his deeds are of no use either to himself or any one else, while he is robbing himself and others of the joy of watching rare birds. Wild swans are always a question. Are they legitimate game? They are not very good to eat and they do not look pretty when dead; while they are beautiful when alive and their music is most enjoyable. Yet, in spite of this, who can fail to be impressed by Colonel Peter Hawker's tale of the shooting of the whoopers?

Mute swans are a different thing altogether. Being more or less protected by law they have bred and multiplied out of all proportion. Where they get on to Zostera beds they ruin them. Where they are very numerous they eat all the duck food and drive away the duck. But in a frost they are useful because they keep a pool

" A DEAD WHOOPER IS NOT BEAUTIFUL. "

[*p.* 80

free from ice; periodically flapping round and round breaking the young ice as it forms. Personally I think that mute swans should always be kept within limits. However that is not a matter which affects the shore shooter, but one for the inland shooter.

CHAPTER V

GEESE

Of the ten species of geese which are known to have visited the British Isles, six are regular visitors coming each year. The other four are accidental visitors and are not likely to be met with by the wildfowler. Of the six which are to be found here each winter, only one, the Greylag, breeds here.

The grey geese are often confused, even when the fowler has killed them and has them in his hand, but if this key is used there should be no more confusion.

Colour of Nail at end of Beak	Colour of Feet	Colour of Bill	Species
White	Flesh Pink	Yellow	Greylag
	Yellow	Pearl Pink with some Yellow	Whitefront or Lesser Whitefront
Black or partly Black	Yellow	Pearl Pink with some Yellow	Young Whitefront or Lesser Whitefront
		Coral Pink and Black	Variety of Pinkfoot
	Orange	Orange and Black	Bean
	Flesh Pink	Coral Pink and Black	Pinkfoot

The Lesser White-fronted goose is distinguished from the Common White-fronted goose by the white of the forehead extending back on the crown as far as the level of the eyes in the former, and not so far as the eyes in the latter. This is only so in adult birds. In young ones which lack the white forehead the only difference, besides size which is always misleading, is that when the bill is closed the 'teeth' cannot be seen from the side.

The Snow geese can always be identified by the black tips to the wings. Many people mistake white varieties of geese for snow geese. I have seen white varieties of pink-footed and bernacle geese and have heard of a white greylag, all of which were mistaken for snow geese. Even Aylesbury ducks, which were able to fly, have been reported as snow geese; but two of these paid the extreme penalty and so were proved to be ducks to the astonishment of their shooter.

The two black geese are unmistakable and so is the red-breasted goose.

Young grey geese can always be told from old by the shape of the breast feathers; those of the young being rounded, of the old square ended. Greylag are the largest British geese, though there is very little difference of size between them and Bean. When seen on the ground or flying low, the piebald appearance of their wings is very noticeable. The front edge of the wing is pale blue grey while the remainder is dark grey. These two colours do not merge into each other, but contrast strongly. The grey rump is paler than in other geese. Greylags often have a few dark spots on the breast, and occasionally so many spots as to make the breast appear black. Like all grey geese they often have a narrow band of white feathers at the base of the bill. I used to believe that this white forehead was only found in old birds, but some tame, hand-reared greylags of mine had it in their first autumn. Young birds often have a triangular white patch under the chin. The usual weight of a greylag is 7 to 9 lb. A 12 lb gander is recorded for England while a monstrous fowl of 16½ lb has been recorded in Europe.

Only a few greylag breed in the British Isles : in the Hebrides and the north of the mainland of Scotland. These begin nesting at the end of April. Northern and eastern Europe and Iceland are their main breeding grounds.

The nests which I have found have all been on islands or promontories in fresh water lochs. They are usually well hidden in long heather, and are built of heather, twigs, and grass and lined with down from the goose's breast. The number of eggs is three to seven, rarely more.

The bird usually lies close on the nest, and only gets up when she is quite certain that she has been discovered. When she leaves the nest to feed, she covers her eggs with grass or down.

At one time they nested in the fens of East Anglia, but, like the ruff and the black-tailed godwit, they were reduced to a minimum by the drainage of the fens and then entirely exterminated by sportsmen and collectors.

In June the greylag moults all its flight feathers simultaneously, and so is deprived of flight for about a month, during which time it frequents the most uninhabited places.

The migrant greylag usually arrive in the British Isles in September and October, but many more come from the Continent when there is hard weather. They are numerous in Scotland and on the west coast of northern England, but rare on the east and south coasts of England. Their main food is grass, clover, corn, and beans. They are not as partial to potatoes as the pink-footed geese.

The white-fronted goose is the smallest of the British grey geese, excepting the lesser whitefront. The black bars across the breast, and the white forehead, besides the long wings, are the distinguishing marks of the adults. The usual weight is about $5\frac{1}{2}$ lb. The lesser white-front has proportionately longer wings than the whitefront.

The whitefront breeds in Russia, Siberia, America, and Greenland. The only nest I have seen was in Greenland, the eggs being fresh on 10th June. They arrive in the British Isles in October.

The lesser whitefront breeds in Siberia, Russia, and Lapland, and spends the winter to the east of Europe. The British Isles are far to the west of its normal habitat.

The whitefront feeds almost entirely on grass and clover.

The bean goose is probably as large as the greylag. I have seen one shot which weighed $9\frac{1}{2}$ lb. The orange feet, and black and orange beak, are the distinguishing marks. When seen standing on the ground, they have a much more upright carriage than any of the other geese. Also they look very long and thin, almost snaky. I have mistaken them for cormorants when I have been punting. Their plumage is also darker than that of the other grey geese. When swimming on the water the body appears long and low, the neck is carried straight and upright, and the head is set on at an abrupt right angle. When flying the neck appears much longer than that of other geese.

The bean geese which I have found nesting in Lapland, prefer wooded country for their nests. The eggs are laid in early June. They arrive in the British Isles in October. They prefer the same grassy, boggy, feeding grounds as do the whitefronts.

The pinkfoot is of medium size, averaging about $6\frac{1}{2}$ lb. The two biggest that I have ever shot, I killed with a right and left; they weighed $7\frac{1}{2}$ and 8 lb.

The very short beak is the best distinguishing mark. In the field they have a much paler, bluer colour than the other grey geese. When seen with other geese, they appear much more 'dumpy' and have much shorter legs.

They nest in Spitzbergen, Iceland, and Greenland. I have seen a great many of their nests in Spitzbergen, where they lay their eggs at the beginning of June. They arrive in the British Isles as early as September.

The pinkfoot's beak is never longer than half the length from the back of the head to the tip of the beak.

The colour of the beak of all birds changes very rapidly after death. The colour of a goose's beak will change, on the living bird, according to the time of year and the weather and the feelings of the bird. In May, a greylag's beak is sometimes almost more pink than yellow.

When the moult comes, in June, their beaks
become an anæmic yellow, all the pink colour
having disappeared. In a sharp frost a Whitefront's beak may appear almost coral red; the
cold seems to affect it in the same way as it affects
some human noses.

The colour of the feet also changes, but to a
lesser extent. Here again, the breeding season
and the temperature are the factors which produce
the change.

The general colouring of the plumage of all
the grey geese is so variable that it is not enough
whereby to identify them. When two, or more,
species are feeding together, it is a help to identi-
fication, but no more.

The call notes of all four of the common grey
geese overlap each other. The deeper notes of
the pinkfoot are almost the same as the higher
notes of the greylag. The higher notes of the
pinkfoot are the same as the deeper notes of the
whitefront. Neither pinkfoot nor whitefront
can make so deep a note as that of the greylag.
Neither greylag nor pinkfoot can make so high
a note as that of the whitefront. The bean goose
is a very silent bird. Its cries are half-way between
those of the greylag and the pinkfoot. It has
one, unmistakable note which is very much
more gruff and hoarse than that of any other
goose.

The calling of grey geese is usually termed
'honking'. Strong powers of imagination are
needed to hear a grey goose say 'Honk'. Nearly
always, the cry of the grey goose is bisyllabic
while that of a black goose is monosyllabic.
But even our own black geese do not say 'Honk'.
The brent says 'Crank' and rolls the 'r', while
the bernacle says 'Yi'. The Canada goose
does make a noise like 'Honk', and perhaps
that is the cause of all the 'honking' in the
wildfowl books. The actual calls of our grey
geese are much more like : 'Ga-ga,' 'Ngu-ngu,'
'Ya-ya,' 'Wa-wa.'

The reason for a wedge or skein formation
is not that it lessens the wind resistance. The
geese have a leader who is responsible for the
direction and altitude of the flock. If the flock
formed a straight line at right angles to their
course, the 'leader' would not be in front.
If they flew in 'line ahead' all except the leader
would be flying through a disturbed atmosphere,
which is known to be a bad medium for flight.
If they flew in a gaggle they would not know
which was their leader nor would all birds be at
the same altitude. When flying very short
distances, or over ground on which other geese
are and they consider there is no danger, they
do fly in a leaderless gaggle. In fact the wedge
and arc formations which they use are the only

ones which enable them to have a leader and to fly through an atmosphere which has not been disturbed by another bird in front of them. I have never seen geese flying in 'line ahead' as many authors say they do. Often they fly in a straight line which, at first sight, appears to be 'line ahead', but is actually one arm of a V, which, due to the drift of the wind, appears to be a 'line ahead'. The changes of leadership which are sometimes witnessed are probably due to the two leaders having a pilot's certificate for different territories. They cannot be due to the leader's getting tired because of his facing the greatest wind resistance, as that is a fallacy. The leader is not always an old bird. Once I shot at the leader of a small wedge of greylags and hit him in the lungs. The wedge had been coming in from the sea, at morning flight. The leader turned and headed back for the sand, his followers keeping their formation. Then the leader began to tower and his followers tried to do the same, but the angle was much too steep for them. Then the leader fell and the flock tumbled after him and almost settled on the sand round him. The leader was a young gander of that year's breeding.

For some years certain periodicals have been constantly publishing lists of 'correct' names whereby to designate flocks of different birds and beasts. All of these lists give the definition of 'skein' as a flock of geese in flight and a 'gaggle' as a flock of geese on the ground. Anyone with the barest knowledge of geese could not call a disorderly flying mob a 'skein'. A 'skein' is obviously the correct word for designating the aggregation of wedges, while no better word than 'gaggle' could be found or invented to describe the loudly calling, flying flock which has no ordered formation. Personally I prefer to go even further and talk of : a 'wedge', meaning a single wedge or V, a 'skein' meaning a more complicated figure consisting of more than one wedge, a 'gaggle' meaning a disordered mob, and a 'flock' when the birds are on the ground.

Chapter VI

GOOSE SHOOTING

The grey geese and the bernacle goose feed mostly by daylight or moonlight. At the time of full moon, if the sky is clear enough to let through sufficient moonlight, the geese feed at night. When there is no moonlight they feed by day. In places where they are seldom disturbed they feed more by day, even when there is bright moonlight at night. The reverse is also true; where they are much disturbed they will come into the fields and feed by starlight.

They use mostly fields which have little cover for hiding a gun, but the popular idea that they always avoid hedges and ditches is a fallacy. I have known a large flock of pink-footed geese to fly twenty miles inland every morning for nearly a week and to settle in an eight acre field surrounded by a tall thorn hedge. The crop was winter wheat on a last season's potato bottom. The whole of the twenty mile course lay over similar crops, in fields of which few were less than fifty acres, many over a hundred, and practically none had hedges. Another time I have seen about two thousand pinkfoots on a stubble

field. Scarcely one of them was more than forty
yards from the ditch, and many were actually in
the bottom of the ditch.

When geese are flighting they nearly always
increase their altitude on coming to a hedge,
dyke, or bank; therefore, if other cover is
procurable, the shooter should take it.

Geese should never be shot on the sand or
mud where they rest, or they will be driven away.
The geese have learned that over the land they
are in danger from shoulder guns, and within
range of water they are in danger from punt
guns, but they are confident of their safety on
the open mud. Break that confidence and they
will leave you. If too much shooting is done on
their feeding grounds, they will forsake those
fields and go to others in the neighbourhood,
but they will not leave the neighbourhood unless
they can get no peace wherever they go.

For flighting it is usually possible to find suitable
cover or make it with little trouble, but for
shooting on the feeding fields it is essential to
take greater care in the preparation of an ambush.
A bare stubble field, or a field of sprouting corn
does not offer much natural cover. If a pit can
be dug it is undoubtedly the best. Failing a pit,
the ditch or hedge must be used. Occasionally
there are other forms of cover which the geese
are used to seeing in the neighbourhood;

agricultural implements, drinking troughs, hurdles, or even scarecrows can all be used as hides. I do not recommend a galvanized drinking trough for comfort in cold weather, but it is sometimes excellent cover.

If a pit is dug in a field, the earth must be taken away. A farmer once promised to make a pit for a friend. The next evening we went to see the pit and found it had every modern convenience except hot and cold water laid on! One could easily stand in the middle of it, and four people could sit on the benches at the ends, without any heads touching the roof! I believe that many cartloads of earth were removed from this mansion, yet from the outside it was almost invisible. A pit of this size is, of course, quite unnecessary; but there is nothing more inconvenient than a pit which is not deep enough and does not really hide the shooter. If geese circle round before settling, a roof over the pit is essential. A sacking roof can easily be thrown aside when the time comes to shoot.

An ordinary hide is best made of wire netting with straw, grass, or rushes, etc., woven into the meshes. And this type of hide can be most effective if it is hidden amongst rushes or in a hedge or bush, but it is essential that it should be hidden. A pit for flighting where birds only pass over does not need a roof. Either a deeper sitting pit or a long shallow lying pit is quickly dug in sand. The sand dug out is made into a rampart in front. The front side of the rampart must have a gentle slope so as not to cast a shadow.

Wind has a very great influence on all flighting birds, and especially on geese. If geese wish to fly from north to south on a calm day they will follow the line north to south. If there is a west wind they will rise facing to west, then turn to face south when the wind will drift them to east, and they will face west again to settle. The distance they travel into the wind and the amount of downwind drift, depends entirely on the strength of wind and the local geography. The knowledge of the exact flight line can only be gained by experience, and then if the direction or force of the wind changes the gunner will find himself in the wrong position. One must always be prepared to run and intercept a flight line. In dull moonlight it is sometimes possible to run right underneath a flight of geese. In daylight it is possible to run until geese are within a few hundred yards. Even if geese are within two hundred yards it is best to run on for cover, rather than to try to efface oneself on a piece of bare ground.

The available cover on different saltings is often of quite different natures. One salting,

which is a favourite of mine, is intersected by
deep narrow creeks whose banks are covered
with seablite, which grows nearly a foot high.
The cover thus afforded is almost perfect; and
in one or two places is perfect, so that even I,
who am six foot high, can stand upright while
waiting for birds. Within a few miles of this
is another salting whose creeks are all shallow
with sloping banks and very little growth of
seablite. On the former, taking cover presents
no difficulties. On the latter there is always a
little digging to be done. Some salt marshes
have a low, cliff-like edge where they drop
abruptly to the sand. This edge serves as admirable
cover for either flighting or stalking. Where
geese are not much disturbed, the sea wall is
often the best place; it provides good cover
for running behind. But if geese are much shot
at, they seldom come low enough over these
walls or banks.

In the Hebrides and other rocky places there
is seldom much difficulty in finding cover, and
even if there is no cover one can often pretend
to be a rock, with some success.

On one occasion in North Uist I was coming
home from fishing when the keeper saw a flock
of geese heading straight for us. I had a gun;
he had the fishing rod. I was on the heather
and immediately took cover; he was a hundred

yards away on the open stony shore and simply converted himself into an imitation stone. The geese glided over his head within a few feet, and settled in the water just out of range from me. Another time we were snipe shooting when some geese appeared. We were both on an open grass meadow, with no cover as the ditches were brimful of water. But there were some small rocks close to us and the geese failed to differentiate between us and the rocks. They gave me a very easy chance but I only got one, instead of a right and left. We were using a red setter for the snipe shooting and he had taught himself to lie down whenever I took cover, no matter where he was. This was a most useful habit and had added many duck to the bag, but this was the first goose he had seen shot. He had a good long sniff at it, and ever afterwards was delighted with geese, getting very excited whenever he heard them.

These Hebridean greylags, in September and October, had no definite habits. There was plenty of food and thousands of resting places. The cornfields were the least uncertain places to wait for them. They were the hardest geese to get that I have yet met, and we got more by good luck than by good management. Stalking was more successful than flighting, but most stalks were spoiled by other birds or beasts.

There were thousands of hoodie crows there and they often gave the show away. Twice we crawled into a herd of deer which galloped off through the geese. Often, when on the water, there were whooper swans near by. A whooper is a living periscope and one of the most difficult birds to stalk. If there is one in the vicinity when a stalk is in progress, and in Uist there were often anything up to sixty, then it is sure to spot the stalker and give the show away to whatever is being stalked by its extraordinary capacity for 'neck rubbering'.

My best sport with greylag, apart from punting, has been flighting inland. Three of us were staying in a house at the mouth of a large river. The grass saltings came up to within two hundred yards of the door, and the river was even closer. I shall never forget my first night there. Thousands of greylags drifted up with the tide and fed on the grass and washed in the water, their babel of noise keeping us awake far into the night.

Next morning we went only a short way from the house and lined out in a convenient creek. But it was a very calm morning and the geese were mostly too high; we only got one. During the day we had three stalks at small flocks feeding close to a bank. The first stalk was quite without incident; we almost walked up to the geese, but we shot badly and only got two. In the second stalk, the geese walked over the bank and so saw us. The third stalk was at a flock of about sixty birds. The two of us easily got within eighty yards, but it was quite impossible to get further. For three-quarters of an hour we lay and watched them feeding nearer then further and nearer again. Eventually they seemed to show no signs of coming closer so we cautiously raised our guns. A whistle, and up went their heads. The first shot killed one on the ground. The next two were unfortunately aimed at the same bird, which came down winged. The fourth hit a bird which set its wings and glided down some two hundred yards away, where it lay dead.

This was the first day that any of the three of us had shot a greylag. We were all three used to pinkfoots and were much impressed with the way the greylags always deliberated before doing anything. When a pinkfoot sees a man its acts very quickly, though not so quickly as a whitefront; but a greylag, unless in immediate danger, seems to delay its action until it has thought of the probable consequences. Among my tame wild geese the greylag are much the most sensible, tamest, and hardest to catch.

The next day we had an example of the smelling

powers of geese. Many people hold the opinion
that geese cannot smell things; others say that
they have 'good noses'. I have repeatedly
noticed that pink-footed geese wind a man at
distances of less than thirty yards, but seldom
or never at greater distances. On this occasion
two of us were stalking a flock of greylags.
Our only means of approach was up a deep
creek which led straight down wind to within
a few yards of the geese, where it turned back
at an acute angle. Near the geese the creek was
narrow, at our end it was wider, like a funnel.
We were 150 yards away from the geese when
they began to get up in small parties. Personally
I am convinced that our scent blew down the
creek to the geese, and that the funnel shape
of the creek concentrated the scent sufficiently
for the geese to wind us.

When we had arrived here and seen and heard
all the geese, we had thought there were a lot,
but that afternoon we realized there had only
been a few. All the late afternoon and evening,
there was not a hand's breadth of sky that did
not contain at least one skein of geese flying
southwards. From this we inferred that a
change of weather was coming, and, sure
enough, within twenty-four hours it was
snowing and blowing hard enough to sink
the punt and all its gear including the big

gun, which was moored in a sheltered bay of the river.

This storm caused a near-by burn to flood its valley, so the geese mostly left our territory and went there.

Having got permission to go after them, one morning found us lined out across the flooded valley, each hidden behind a gorse bush. There was a thick fog, so only a few geese flighted in at dawn. In the fog they looked much closer than they were and consequently we shot badly. Suddenly a furious gamekeeper arrived on the scene. It appeared that the farmer, who had given us permission to shoot, had no right to do so. As the keeper was going away, to speak to the farmer, some more geese came in. He, like the Scots minister who found a small boy fishing on the Sabbath, immediately joined in the sport which, the moment before, he had been condemning. Suddenly diving under a gorse bush he shouted at us to take cover also. That morning we did not do well, but next morning we waited in the ditch of a meadow where they had been feeding on the previous day. Each of the first two bunches to arrive yielded a right and left. The second two were both runners and needed hunting for with the dogs, as both were among the thick rushes. Whistling soon brought the two dogs from their hiding place

under a bush 200 yards away. But a goose
can run at a surprising speed and by the time the
first was collected, the second had gone two
fields. However, geese usually have a strong
scent and this one was run straight up to by
Trick, the Labrador. Then a single goose
came in and was shot at, but went 400 yards
before collapsing. It was soon found by Pansy,
the spaniel, who, not being large enough to carry
a greylag, bounced about round it in her usual
manner. The last geese to come in were a bunch
of four; three fell and the fourth glided down
into the burn. The burn was still in flood and
we never found this last one.

That evening I winged another goose, which
fell far out on the sand of the estuary, and went
' hirpling ' off at great speed. After a long chase
Trick caught it. Out of the nine geese shot that
day there were five which we should have been
very lucky to get without the aid of a dog.

I have always been unable to understand
the prejudice against dogs while goose shooting,
provided that the dogs are properly trained and
obedient.

On the last day of our stay at this place, we
found a flock of about 200 greylags feeding
on either side of a hedge which divided two
grass fields. A stalk was out of the question
as the hedge was the only cover. So one of us

walked round them at a distance, gradually drawing closer, until those on the near side of the hedge flew over and joined their companions on the far side. They were now all out of range of the hedge, so a drive seemed the only hope. My two companions crawled up the hedge and waited in some gorse bushes, while I walked round the geese. I walked backwards and forwards, whistling, never going directly towards or away from the geese, but keeping them gently walking towards the hedge. Most of the time I was between 200 and 120 yards from them. Whenever they looked as though they were getting too alarmed, I retreated, and when they got too interested in their feed I advanced. Suddenly four shots came from the hedge, and, with a mighty cackling, the geese came straight back to one side of me. I ran under them and also got a chance of a right and left but missed them clean with both barrels, quite inexcusably as they were very close to me.

In this locality the greylags were so used to seeing men working in the fields that they would always allow an indirect approach to within about 200 yards, a few merely lifting their heads and watching the intruder. But any suspicious action caused the whole flock to stop feeding and watch intently, while to disappear into a ditch would cause them to seek their food elsewhere. The bernacle geese had very different habits.

The bernacles lived on the short grass of the sea marsh, roosting on the same sandbars as the greylags. They seldom fed elsewhere than on the salting, and never went any distance inland. Their feeding ground being the strip of salting made it much more difficult to flight them than it was to flight the greylags which flew in on definite lines, the bernacles merely flying on to whatever piece of salting took their fancy. We found the best way of getting at the bernacles was by stalking them when they were feeding, or by getting into position between them and the sea before they flighted out.

Their territory consisted almost entirely of grass cropped so close as to resemble a lawn. The only available cover was the creeks and the little cliff-like edge where the grass gave way to the sand of the open firth. But in some places the grass and sand merging gradually into each other made a break in the cliff.

The greatest asset for stalking was a thorough knowledge of the ground. At first we would see the geese feeding where we thought a creek would lead to them. A laborious crawl for an hour or more might then show that we should have gone up the next creek but one. If we did so, which usually meant a long detour, by the time we reached the place where the geese had been it was ten to one that they had walked away far out of range. We soon found that the bernacle geese are very fast walkers, and that when they are feeding they usually keep going at a considerable speed, the ones at the back often flying up, over their companions, to take their turn in the front rank. It would be hopeless to stalk up to where we had seen them, so we would stalk to get in front of them to some position which we hoped they would pass.

The first successful stalk that I ever had at bernacles took me almost the whole of an afternoon. I was alone on a piece of salt marsh where I had never been before. There were about a hundred geese feeding in an area that I could see was a network of creeks. I went out to the sand about half a mile from them and so got under the edge of the marsh which here was nearly four feet high. By stooping down, I was able to circle back along this edge, until I came to a big creek up which it was possible to walk in an upright position. Coming round a corner of the creek, I put up a redshank which flew off screaming. At once all the geese rose, but only to circle round and settle again in the same place. I resumed my stalk, going more cautiously

for fear of disturbing other redshanks. I was
continually coming to places were tributary
creeks converged, and having to choose which
one to follow. Often I took the wrong one, and
had to retrace my steps and try another. Then the
creeks got shallower and shallower the further
I went up them ; from stooping I had to go on
hands and knees. Then another cursed redshank
tried to settle on me, saw me and made enough
noise to waken the dead. Up got the geese and
flew into an area which was drained by another
creek system.

This necessitated returning almost to the open
sand before finding a creek running in the right
direction. Then the whole stalk started again,
but by the time I had reached the head of the
creek the geese had fed away out of shot. I was
completely blown, because, forseeing this, I had
been racing to try and get there while they were
still within range ; so I lay down to rest.

When I next looked at the geese the last
ones were just walking away over a very slight
ridge. This was my opportunity for doing a flat
belly crawl down a slight depression which led
to the head of another creek, and dropping into
it without being seen. Then it appeared that by
going down it, and up the next, I should be able
to get a shot, but as I reached the junction there
was a greenshank wading in the bottom. I have

never had such a close view of a greenshank, but still I cursed it heartily. It flew off but, unlike the redshanks, it did not call its alarm note until it had gone about fifty yards. The geese this time moved right away from me and I thought I had seen the last of them.

They settled some way off but in such a position that it appeared extremely likely that they would flight out past me when the time came; so I waited where I was. Close beyond them was the sea wall, to one side some gorse bushes, to the other side a wide creek with a farmhouse beyond it. They seemed to dislike their position and began walking back towards me. I crawled as close as I could and waited. In half an hour their leaders were within shot, but still I waited for their ranks to come on. But they had finished feeding by then, and were sitting down and preening their feathers, so came no closer. The light was failing fast, and it would soon have been difficult to see them on the ground, so at length I fired at them. There were three together, which I tried for with the first barrel; but one of them was only wounded, so I had to give it the second barrel.

Another season, on this same marsh, I spent a whole morning stalking a very large flock of bernacles. They were put up by redshanks three times, once they saw me, and once a hoodie

crow flying over spotted me. The crow made no
sound, but suddenly backed away and swerved.
That was enough for the geese though, and they
went straight out on to the sand as frightened
as though they had been shot at.

This is a peculiarity of the bernacles; that
they will see a man stalking them and not be
greatly alarmed, yet the sight or sound of another
bird which has itself been alarmed will put them
up at once. Sometimes it seemed as though
their jumpiness was simply 'reflex action',
because they would settle again in exactly the
same place from which they had jumped.

The only other place where I have tried to shoot
bernacles was in the Outer Hebrides. Here
their territory was quite unlike the ground which
I have just described. A multitude of small
rocky islands with sheep-bitten grass provided
them with both feeding and resting places.
Some of these islands had rock cliffs dropping
sheer into the sea, others sloped up gently from
the water's edge; some were only a few yards
in each direction, while others were many
acres in extent; and some had long heather
and peat hags, while others were devoid of
all cover.

There were so many islands that it was purely
a matter of luck if the geese came to an island
on which one of us had landed; so we soon

SETTING OUT

gave up trying to flight them. The most profitable, or, rather, least unprofitable plan was to stalk and drive them. Sometimes the dinghy would go and lie under a cliff while the motorboat went to the other side of the island and tried to drive the geese over it. Sometimes one gun went to each of the most likely of the neighbouring islands while another gun waited for them to get to their respective places, then tried to stalk the geese.

On one such occasion I was the gun who was to stalk the geese. Just before I left the motorboat I asked if there were any sheep on the island. Angus replied that there were none, so I knew there was no chance of crawling on top of one and sending it galloping madly into the geese, which is what I had done a few days before. As I saw the motor-boat take the last of my companions to his island, I began the stalk. The whole time while I waited, I could hear the bernacles on the top of the island, about 60 feet above me and 300 yards away. Making sure that there were no large gulls anywhere near me, I walked up to a rock near the top and spied round it. There was nothing to be seen, but the noise of the geese sounded very close over the hill. I dare not look over the top of the rock because my head would have been silhouetted against the sky. As in deerstalking, so with geese this

is usually fatal to success. To one side of me
was a bank, overgrown with long heather, which
I could easily reach. After crawling a short
way amongst the heather I came in sight of the
farthest geese. The nearer ones were out of sight
below me, hidden by the edge of the ground which
I lay on. If I was to crawl on I should be in full
view of the far geese all the way, whereas I could
go back round the shore and come up underneath a rock ledge, which was within shot of
the geese. Apparently it was possible to walk
the whole way, only having to stoop in one
place.

My rubber boots were almost silent on the
rocks, which, being dry, were not slippery. At
one place I had to climb across a rock face which
only had a crack a few inches wide. If the rock
had been wet I should not have tried it, as it was,
it was not too easy with a gun in one hand and
wearing thick-soled thigh boots. A seal came
bobbing along underneath me, much interested
until he got my wind. I reached my ledge without
any difficulty and was intent on preparing to
look over. The sound of the geese came from
so close above me that I was sure that they were
within range. Suddenly there was a loud ' Gor,
gor ' from over my head. The goose noises
stopped and then, at once, I heard their wings.
Leaping up the rocks I fired both barrels at the

last bird, but they had gone too far in the short time that it took me to get in sight of them. It was another spoiled stalk to go to the account of the black-backed gulls. The geese, as usual, chose to settle on one of the many islands where there was no waiting gun.

CHAPTER VII

GOOSE SHOOTING (*continued*)

Most of my goose shooting has been done on
the East Coast of England, where the commonest
geese are pink-footed.   Some white-fronted
geese and a very few bean geese accompany
the pinkfoots, but greylag are extremely rare.

When these geese first arrive, in October,
they resort to the stubbles and clover leys for
their food.   Later on they leave the stubbles
and go to the potato fields and grass marshes.
Winter wheat sprouting on a 'taty bottom',
is perhaps their favourite feeding ground ; here
they can have alternate mouthfuls of nice soft
potato and luscious green wheat blades.   It is
only of quite recent years that the large flocks of
geese have been going to a certain potato and
wheat country.   When they first started, the
farmers were horrified to see their winter wheat
eaten right down, and, thinking their crops would
be ruined, paid men to scare the geese.   Now
most of these farmers realize that no harm is
done, some even saying that they get far heavier
crops from the fields which the geese have
eaten down and manured.

In severe frosts the potatoes get frozen so hard that the geese have difficulty in nibbling them, and so desert the potato fields and go to the clover leys, the grass marshes, or the grass-covered saltings.

My best bags have usually been made when geese were going on to the potato bottoms, and when they were feeding by moonlight rather than daylight.

One such night, after the full of the moon, two of us, P. and I, waited out for the flight which we expected to begin any time after moonrise. We had been out on the saltings' edge flighting the mallard as they came in at dusk. Then, when it became dark, we returned to the sea wall and sat down under the shelter of it to wait and listen for the goose flight. There were no stars visible, because of the overcast sky, and the moon did not appear, though the sky did get a bit lighter. An acquaintance, who had joined us while duck flighting and decided to wait for the geese with us, got up and went home to his supper, saying he thought it was a " very poor flight to-night ". We saw the headlights of his car go on and turn in the stack-yard and start away down the road, and at the same time we heard geese moving. Before those headlights were out of sight we were running down under the bank, trying to get in front of

H

the incoming geese. We stopped, and as the direction of the noise seemed coming straight for us, one went on, the other back. P. had them right over him and got one. I went to pick it up and had not regained the wall when we heard another lot. Then for the next two hours we were running up and down the wall, sometimes failing to judge right or run quick enough, at other times being lucky and getting under the birds. Often they were too high and we did not fire, but sometimes they were low enough and sometimes there was a small bunch flying low and silent behind one of the high skeins. After some while geese began flying out to sea again, although the inward flight was not yet over. Presumably they wanted a drink to wash down their meal. There was more than one occasion when I had to decide which lot of geese to try to get under. After much practice it is possible to decide from the noise alone whether geese are high or low, but in those days we were yet unable to do so. The dog, as always, was a great help. But I lost some chances through having to take Pansy to look for P's birds, as he had no dog of his own. We shot none too well, but we finished the flight with twelve geese.

Another time, in January, four of us went to the same place intending to shoot the geese from the ditch of a potato field. But on arriving we found that we had been forestalled and that three other people had shot them there two nights before. We changed our plans and went to the sea wall once more. There was a bad sky for shooting and we shot abominably, getting only two geese, both pinkfoots. We stayed out all night, got miserably cold and tired, and shot no better.

Then, after some sleep in a straw stack, we went out on the salting for a morning flight. Here P. got a very fine bean goose, which weighed 9½ lb, and R. got two pink-footed geese and lost a wigeon. The other two of us got nothing.

After a late breakfast we slept until it was time for a late lunch, after which we went out again. According to my diary, " We found a perfectly frightful woman shooting with a fat boy and a lunatic man and accompanied by another bird-scaring bag-carrying woman. They apparently intended staying here so we told them as many lies as we could think of and then went out on to the saltings." This was not a very charitable thing either to do or to write of ; but we had to use every means to protect our shooting grounds from becoming too well known. Just before it began to get dark some geese came in high over me. I had a shot and did not get the one I aimed at, nor even the one behind it, but I winged the one behind that. Then at evening flight P. and I each got a wigeon. In the space between evening flight and moonrise we all had to walk about to keep warm.

Then the moon rose. The sky was very different from that of the previous night; only one long low dark cloud, the rest of it white from the thin fleecy clouds. As soon as the moon looked over the top of the low dark cloud, the geese began moving. I heard P. have two shots and then have words with Darky, the dog I had lent him. Knowing that Darky was pretty useless I went over to see if I could help him. He was outside the edge of a quickly rising tide and unable to find either of a right and left of geese. All the surrounding water was dotted with lumps of plants, each of which was the size and shape of a goose and each of which needed his close scrutiny, because Darky, deeply shocked by the language, had departed to the dry land. Pansy soon caught one, a runner, while P. found the other.

We were splashing shorewards, the tide having risen some way, when P. suddenly fired. I whirled round and had a snap shot at some geese which were just disappearing behind me. One slanted away from the others, and I sent Pansy after it. She got it, 300 yards away, at the tide edge. It was a young whitefront.

The flowing tide, forcing us all to retreat,

brought M. to join us. All three of us had a few
more shots at geese, but without any success.
Then we all three started out to look for a bird
which we thought we had heard fall after one
of my shots. In the first few steps M. sat down
in a creek, so went straight back to the car to
change his clothes. We soon found the goose,
a fine old whitefront with wide black bars on his
breast. After a little longer we returned to the
car for supper and then home. We felt that we
had done extremely well. Though our bag was
not very great—eight geese—it contained three
species: bean, whitefronts, and pinkfoots. The bean
goose was the second that we had ever shot and
the two whitefronts were the first that we had
shot on this marsh. And that reminds me of the
peculiar way that luck had run with us all on this
particular marsh up to last year (1935). I was the
only one to have shot whitefronts here, P. had
the monopoly of beans, D. of brents, and A.
of bernacle. And this in spite of the fact that
every year there are some beans, and some whitefronts, and every year of hard weather there are
brents, though the bernacle must have been
an accidental visitor to this marsh which has
little in common with the kind of ground they
prefer.

On this saltmarsh we used to get most of our
geese at morning flight, as they came in from the

sand bars and passed over to the potato fields. At certain times of the season, especially in frosty weather, they would come to this salting to feed on the grass, and then was the occasion for good sport. But whatever the weather or where-ever the geese were feeding, there was always a fair chance of getting one or two and a few duck.

One night in February, within a few days of the end of the season, P. and I waited for the geese to come in under the moon to a farm some twenty miles from our salting. The geese chose that night to go elsewhere, so, being tired of waiting by soon after midnight, we also went away. We left our car in the stackyard of a farm and walked down towards the sea wall. When we had gone half the way we heard the quiet, contented noise of geese which have satisfied their hunger but are still resting on their feeding place. We had suspected right; the geese had come to this potato field.

We settled down and made ourselves comfort-able in the loose straw at the end of a potato grave. As we lay and dozed and talked we could hear the geese all round us and so made sure of their numbers and disposition. As the night came to its coldest, which is usually about three or four in the morning, we were no longer warm. The straw was not deep enough and the dogs were not large enough or hairy enough to cover us both, so we decided to go off and try for the duck which usually came at about this time to a pool of fresh water. We were unfortunate, and failed to see the only pair of ducks which were on the pool.

As the flight time drew near we went out on the salting. There had been a north-east wind all night and now it turned itself into a strong blizzard. The darkening sky had obscured the moonlight and the dawn was barely commencing, when geese began flighting out from the fields. Probably it was the increased darkness which made them start so early.

I was only half-way to where I had intended taking my position, when some geese suddenly called from close behind me. They came straight over me, low as anyone could wish for, and beating slowly into the wind. So slowly they came, that I poked at them and missed with both barrels. Within a minute another lot came and I missed them, then a third lot and I only got one. Other geese were passing wide to my front. Then three passed me wide to one side, turned, and came back straight for me with the wind in their tails. There was no time to poke and my first barrel killed two of them, astonishing me so much that I missed the third. I had then had nine shots, and only hit with two of them, so I was not too well pleased with myself. Then the geese seemed to avoid me, passing just out of range to one side or the other, often right over the position I had been in a few minutes before. The wind was so squally that it gave their flight a zigzag course, making it impossible to reckon where they would pass. A single goose came out and settled 200 yards from me. I stalked it and got it.

When P. and I rejoined each other at the sea wall, all the geese had flighted out. He had been right off the flight line and only got one mallard. A small party of brent geese had come up with the rising tide and fed slowly towards him, but he had been flooded out of his creek before they came within range.

Quite a lot of snow fell during the day, and the wind kept up its force. As we went out again for the evening flight, we looked to the south-west and saw a white country, to the north-east and saw a brown one with little white in its make up ; the snow was piled on the windward side of everything.

I got three wigeon and a curlew, walking them up in the narrow creeks, before it was flight time. At dusk the tide, driven in early by the storm, washed the geese off their sand bar. They came in to the saltings, all in one big mob, and I only got one of them. Then it became too dark to see and I returned to the sea wall once more. P. had again had no luck, getting only a mallard and a dunlin. I had had all the luck this day, and had made bad use of it. Not very long before, the weights had been in the other scale and I had had to help carry P's geese.

We had wished to wait out this night in the potato field where we had heard the geese the previous night, but one side of each furrow was brown, and the other white with snow, and we realized that it was impossible to hide ourselves, so spent the night in bed and did some sleeping for a change.

This same spell of hard weather caused the shallow water of the mudflats to freeze and the snow to freeze on to them as the tide ebbed. Then as the tide flowed again it took these pans of ice, lifted them from the mud and jostled them against each other until each slipped under or over its neighbour, so forming cakes of ice. Then the action of sun and wind, spray and frost, made them into miniature icebergs. The high water mark became a wall of jumbled bergs and floes, while large flat pans of ice drifted up on the tide, covered with ranks of weary, starving dunlins and knots. All the geese went into the grass fields where the snow lay thinly, and there they stayed night and day while the snow lasted, not flighting at all. The snow on the ground made the nights light, so the geese felt secure in their ability to see all intruders, in spite of the moonless nights.

The first morning of these conditions, before the geese had left the sea, three of us went out for the flight. We arrived none too early and then found the salting covered with 2 feet of slush. The last high tide had brought up all the snow from the mudflats and deposited it on the salting, where it had not yet frozen. It was impossible to hurry, when every step went through to the hard ground below. The geese began going inland when we were still some way from our places. Then we came to a patch of pack ice, and here M. stayed, well hidden behind an upturned slab of ice. Then P. found a creek where the bare mud showed brown and there he waited. I had a white kennel coat and a white balaclava helmet and so went out on the bare mud and tried to look like a piece of ice. The geese entirely failed to notice me until I moved to fire. Then they also moved, and with no hesitation, presenting shots that were by no means easy ones. Some of them would simply dive straight at me and then go away twisting like snipe. I shot abominably and only got one pinkfoot and a wigeon. M. got a whitefront and a pinkfoot, while P. was avoided by all the geese.

It is not always wintry weather when goose

shooting is possible.   I can remember times
when I have been burned by the sun or bitten
by midges, while lying waiting for geese.   One
time in early autumn two of us received word that
the pinkfoots were arriving.   We took ourselves,
with all speed, to the marsh which we knew
they would go to.   Here we met two other friends,
so all set out together at six o'clock in the evening.
P. and I went to one place while the other two
went to another.

At the place which we chose, a creek flowed
out from the salting, and had formed a large
bay of open sand.   At the edges of the bay
the salting culminated abruptly in a little cliff
which dropped vertically to the sand   below.
This little cliff was anything from 1 to 4 feet high
and made excellent hiding places.   I found a
place where the edge had been washed away
so as to form a little bay, no bigger than a grouse
butt.   Here I was perfectly hidden from three
sides, while the background would probably
serve to conceal me from birds coming on the
fourth side.   The cliff edge was 3 ft high, so
it was as perfect a hide as I could wish for.   There
was a nice warm wind and the sand was dry,
making it, altogether, a very comfortable place
to wait in ;   but there was seldom any waiting
to be done.   Geese were passing in all directions
and at all heights.   Newly arrived birds came in

high and dropped down to their companions either on the sand or on the grass and birds which had probably arrived earlier in the day flew from one flock to another. There was no regular flight, but a vast concourse of geese in big flocks and little flocks, family parties, pairs and single birds; thousands, hundreds, tens, and ones. Although they passed in all directions, the birds flying from the grass and going out on to the sand were the most numerous, and my place was right on their line of flight. Most of them were too high to shoot at, but many were well within range and a few were really low.

There were so many birds about that I often watched the wrong ones and so let others go by within shot. At one time I had five down as quickly as I could load; two rights and lefts of high birds straight over my head and a single one low to the right. We had taken so long getting here that we had little more than an hour of shooting. In that time I got twelve geese, all pinkfoots, and was so busy attending to my own business that I saw little of what P. was doing. But I did see one perfect right and left of birds that were well up in the air and both killed clean and falling stone dead within a few yards of each other.

When it became too dark to shoot we rejoined

each other and I found that P. had got eight birds. He had not found such an ideal position as I had found, and the bulk of the outward flight had missed him. We had a weary, but happy, three miles in the dark, each carrying ten geese. The other two had got five geese between them.

All the geese we got, and saw or heard, were pink-footed geese. I had never seen so many geese, or even dared to think of so many. That night I wrote in my diary: "At one time there must have been ten thousand in the air at once, and the full complement must have been nearly twenty thousand, or maybe even more." We arrived at these approximate figures by counting the individual birds in one section of a flock, then estimating how many similar sections there were in the flock. We doubted our own figures and so counted again and again.

CHAPTER VIII

FRESH MARSH SHOOTING

The best method of working private duck shoots depends on the type of shooting ground. Some small pools or rivers may be shot once every ten days, while other large broads or marshes are best left undisturbed and only shot three or four times in each season. Broadly speaking, a feeding place, where the shooting is done at evening flight, may be shot far more often than a resting place, where the shooting is done at morning flight.

Duck choose a resting place because of its security from danger. They associate quietness with security. If the quietness is constantly broken the duck forsake the place, so it is best to be very careful not to shoot too often and, when shooting, not to stay too late. If the last few lots of duck are allowed to come in undisturbed they, at least, will return again and so attract others.

Evening flighting is different in that the late arrivals cannot be seen in the darkness and so are always allowed to come in. Hence the reason that feeding places can be shot more often than resting places.

A resting place can be shot, by means of 'stirring it up' in the daytime, quite often; whereas morning flighting it the same number of times would drive away all the duck, if the shooting is carried on until the end of the flight.

On really large marshes certain pools and corners can be flighted without disturbing the rest of the place, but I think it is best seldom, or never, to flight the whole marsh with a number of guns, certainly not more than five times a season.

The requirements of a resting place for duck are open water, shelter, and lack of disturbance, also a little food, sufficient for an occasional snack, and some dry banks to rest on. The water must be still, or comparatively so, and preferably not very deep. Shelter of small reed beds, willows, and alders is ideal. Large reed beds are a nuisance in every way. If there is water of about one or 2 ft depth, free from reeds, some of our many native duck foods will grow there. Where there are dry banks they are always used by ducks to rest on and sun themselves. Where there are no natural banks, artificial ones are easily made in the reed beds. The reeds on the south side of a bed are cut in the form of a bay, and heaped up on top of the still standing reeds in the centre of what then becomes the south side. Thus a nice bank is formed, facing south and sheltered from the other three sides. In the same way, beautifully sheltered pools can be made in the middle of large reed beds, the reeds being piled on the north sides of the cuttings to form the sunny banks. If there is sufficient space other bays and banks should be made facing east and west, so as to catch the morning and evening sun, though the flanks of the bays which face south, serve this purpose. The droppings and feathers which soon accumulate on the banks show that they are appreciated.

In making these cuttings all food plants should be left uncut. The seeds of yellow flags, crowfoots, and bedstraws and many other plants are eaten by ducks ; while the submerged pondweeds, duckweed, crowfoots, and starworts are all eaten. In chalk streams the water celery and watercress are as valuable to the duck shooter as to the trout fisher. Not only do the ducks eat the plant, but innumerable snails and insect larvæ, which live on it, are eaten by the ducks. All these plants should be encouraged. Reeds should be kept within bounds ; small beds being excellent cover but large beds being quite useless. If reeds can be cut under water in July and early August they can be killed. But they must be cut

at this time and the cut must be under water or
they will not be killed. This is not so easy in
practice as on paper, as in these months the reed
beds are so often high and dry above the summer
level of the water. If they are submerged it is no
easy matter to cut them. Arm a novice with a
scythe, put him to work in the water and watch
the performance. One moment up comes the
blade and skims the surface, next it is looking
for eels in the mud; the slightest deviation
making the blade go astray. Personally I find a
Highland Scotch scythe handle infinitely superior
to an English one for this job and for any other
really rough work. Of course, no English
labourer would be seen dead in a ditch with
one, they are much too conservative and
will only use the tools which their forefathers
used.

Wire netting, suitably placed near the butts,
is a great help to cripple chasing. The wire can
be erected at the same time as the reed cutting
is done. After a shoot, the cripple chasing
can be done in such a way as to drive the
cripples up to the wire, then along it into a
corral.

The making of artificial places for duck depends
so much on the location and locality that it is
impossible to generalize about them. The
maintenance of all duck preserves depends on

I

the correct balancing of open water and shelter, the admission of sunlight and exclusion of wind, and the presence of suitable food plants.

Nature is always trying to level everything; to fill up the swamps and raze off the hills. Most

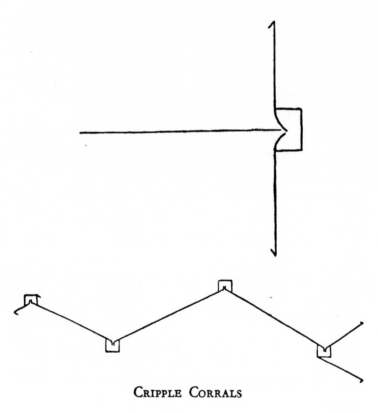

CRIPPLE CORRALS

of her works are infinitely slow, but the filling up of swamps is one of her quickest. The superabundance of reeds is her first move in this direction, if left alone they will be followed by willows and alders, if removed they can be replaced by useful open water and food plants.

My earliest attempts at flighting, and many others since then and up to the present date, were done on a Hampshire chalk stream. The stretch of water which holds duck is sheltered on both sides by alder, willow, and sallow, and reeds and sedges. The current of water is slow because it is held up by a grinding mill at the lower end of the stretch. There is always a good depth of water because one of the largest springs in the county is at the head of the stretch. Food plants grow in abundance and the place is kept quiet. The duck population at its lowest ebb is about twenty, while in hard weather there may be as many as 300. If the alders are allowed to get too high the duck do not like it; rising and landing become difficult, and the shade shuts out sunlight; so periodically the alders have to be cut. Then the duck do not like it because of the lack of privacy. Besides the river itself there are some little pools and springs, which hold duck. These are continually being choked by vegetation of all kinds, and so become useless for duck unless constantly opened up.

The ducks are composed almost entirely of mallard, with a very few teal—one wigeon and one shoveller have been shot in the last twenty years.

For shooting this place in the daytime three guns are required, a greater number is not so good. Number one is put in his place with orders not to shoot until 'zero hour', unless all the duck get up before then. Numbers two and three have to combine the offices of forward guns and beaters. As no gun can see either of the others all must have synchronized watches. Two minutes before zero hour numbers two and three get within thirty yards of their objectives, so that if things go wrong they can run to their posts. At zero hour each creeps into his position and tries for a shot at the duck as they rise, and, incidentally, each sends the duck to the other and to number one. Shooting is all over in a few minutes, except for the chance of some of the duck dropping in again. After waiting for this chance, number two works his dogs through the small pools and the reeds on the banks, thereby sometimes putting up some more duck. The bag varies from none to a record of fourteen, anything over six being considered good. Long practice has proved that the duck will stand this treatment once a fortnight throughout the whole season. In February they are all paired, and so then they are left alone, while they are not usually shot till after the middle of August.

Trials of flighting have proved that the duck will not stand it nearly as often as the method described above. More duck are killed at the first few flights, but after that there may be no duck to kill. The best method is to flight only when there are large numbers of duck present, using a daytime 'stir up' as the normal method.

One morning of hard frost, as a small boy, armed with a twenty-bore and accompanied by my father's Labrador, I met the keeper and his dog before the first light. We waded, through the ice-bound reeds, to the river's bank. Some ducks rose, quacking, from almost under our feet, their white tails visible against the dark alders. *Bang, bang*; and one splash told of a fallen duck. This was soon collected and we walked down the bank to a butt made of two hurdles and a growing sallow bush. This butt had an excellent floor which was really a nest made by a swan in the previous spring. The wind was strong and blowing down stream, so it would be in the face of the ducks as they flew up from the Test valley. Eagerness had made me come out much too early, but there was a lot to hear and a little to see, the remains of a late moon shining dimly through the thin clouds. Moorhens and dabchicks were waking up and calling, the laughing of the latter sounding very loud. Some pigeons, two cock pheasants, and a party of jays began making subdued noises from the alders. The cocks in the village had been crowing for some time. Two dabchicks floated down within a few feet without noticing the intruders. Suddenly the dogs showed great interest in the wind. A moment later I saw a small log floating down the stream. It came abreast of me and sank; then I realized it was an otter. The dogs suppressed their excitement with difficulty.

A quacking from downstream heralded the first lot of ducks, which were missed with both barrels. Then one was killed from a pair coming over high, then two more misses at a lot dropping vertically downwards. After this a long time with no ducks coming and plenty of thought on the wasted opportunities, for one duck with six shots was certainly not very good. The keeper said he thought it was a waste of time shooting at duck which were ' falling ' in, much better wait and shoot when they flattened out before landing, or after they had landed !

A party of teal suddenly appeared and one fell into the bushes Then five ducks flying low straight up the river. Up came the gun and down came two ducks. " A good right and left," the keeper pronounced, and I agreed, but with rather a guilty conscience, as I knew they had both fallen to the second barrel. The next few duck were handsomely missed and then, as the light improved, I began to deal with them as I should. But by then the flight was nearly over. The old barn owl flew across the river to his home in the top of the mill. In a few more minutes the sun was almost showing, and then I went to look for the teal. As the dog went into the bush something got up with a whirr. It was almost hidden by the mass of twigs, but the shot got it and the dog ran in and brought it back : a woodcock. Then he returned into the bush and got the teal. I came back to the river bank with a cock teal in one hand and a woodcock in the other. I could not decide which was the more beautiful and kept looking at them and wondering. Then I saw the mallards, nine of them, lying in the butt, and wondered why I should not have thought of the drakes as being equally beautiful and supposed it was because they were more familiar to me.

A short walk through the rushy meadows in search of snipe completed the early morning excursion and I went home to breakfast.

For many years this alder fringed river was the only real duck shooting available to me, not counting the few ducks occasionally met with while game shooting. Then I discovered that ducks could be shot in the most unfavourable looking places. Really they only had the appearance of being unfavourable to one who did not know. Dry, upland, stubble fields and little ponds in the oak woods.

Now, although all this may have been shooting ducks, it is doubtful if it was duck shooting and it certainly was not wildfowling. The real opportunities for wildfowling first came my way when I was an undergraduate at Cambridge: excursions frequently to the flooded fens, and less often to the sea coast. Then came expeditions in the vacation, with friends, to parts of our coasts farther afield. And so, by degrees, I became a wildfowler. Then my friends and I began to acquire bits of duck shooting in various places and I have been very fortunate in having had some extremely good days on these shoots.

A Norfolk marsh, in which I had a share, is situated close inside the sea wall. The marsh itself is flooded with fresh water, and so is a great attraction to the fowl from the bay. Our best sport used to be with the teal in the late autumn. Flighting in the early morning was the most successful.

One morning, in the middle of October, three guns met the watcher at the roadside. As we got out of our cars we realized that the wind was much stronger than we had thought, and blowing in such a way as to head the incoming birds. By the time we had our thigh boots on it was already five o'clock, and we should have been in position by then. On the way across the intervening fields, a few duck and snipe could be heard getting up from the water splashes, plovers were flying round everywhere. When we reached the punt, the watcher, and A., and his spaniel embarked in it. They had to get round a deep stretch of water that could not be waded. S. and myself went on foot towards our places. Quantities of coots scuttered off across the open water to their sanctuary in the big reed bed, and a few ducks also rose and disappeared in the darkness. They had been on the feeding bank stealing the barley which was thrown there for the duck.

A hundred yards through knee-deep water brought us to S's butt; a screen built of reeds in the edge of a reed bed. Another eighty yards brought me to my butt; another reed screen in a small clump of reeds. As I reached my butt two shots sounded from the boat and a panic-stricken mass of ducks flew out past me. I had three shots and got only one bird, which fell on the dry bank where I had told my dogs to stay and so was easily retrieved. By this time A. was in his butt, eighty yards or so beyond me, and had started shooting. A's butt was on a small dry island surrounded by knee deep water in which grew a lot of sedge. Upwind

of it was a fair sized pool of open water; some
way downwind was a reed bed. The two other
butts were on a dryish bank with a reed bed
close in front. A small pool of open water
lay between and behind them. Except where the
reeds grew all this ground was covered with a
mass of sea aster growing about 2 feet high.
Earlier in the season this was a garden of purple
flowers, like Michaelmas daisies, but now the
silver seeds were ripe and clouds of them were
blowing like thistledown on the wind.

S. was not getting any shooting at all, a few
birds were coming my way, and A. was firing
incessantly. I could not get nearer to him, because
of the deep water. Obviously, from the sound,
there was room for more than one gun where
he was, while S. was right off the flight line. However, my mistake could not now be rectified,
so we must stay in our positions.

The wind was bending the swaying reeds in
front of me, sometimes bowing them almost flat.
And the aster seeds were blowing in such quantities as to fill my eyes and nose if I looked upwind. As the light improved I could see the teal
further out in front; they would rise up and drop
down, disappearing behind the reeds, sometimes
to reappear suddenly when they were already
within shot. The shooting was difficult as some
of the birds would be hanging in the wind while

others were travelling fast.   Second barrels were
mostly at birds being carried up and away.   The
wind was so strong that ears were not of much
assistance.

As the light became really good I could see
flock after flock of teal, creeping up against the
wind, going straight to A.   It was apparent
that he would soon be running short of cartridges and also that his dog would have more than
enough work, so I set off on the detour to reach
him, sending S. to take my place.   It was a long
detour, and by the time I reached him the main
flight was as good as finished.   He had over
fifty birds down, so we immediately set to work
to pick them up.   He had already picked a good
many with his dog.

While we worked our dogs we would get an
occasional shot at birds coming in and at those
which settled to the side and could be walked
up.   I was stooping to take a cock wigeon from
one Spaniel, at the same time watching the other
which had a winged teal in a clump of sedge,
when I heard a 'look out' whistle.   Dropping
into the cover as best I could without submerging,
I looked up and saw five birds wheeling towards
me.   The dawn light shone brightly on them;
three wigeon and two pintail.   They were passing
upwind of me when I rose to fire.   On seeing
me they swerved downwind and over me;

my first barrel, going off as they swerved, had no effect. The drake pintail fell to the second barrel. He was only winged so I put the dogs on him straight away, but one had already got a live, winged teal and the other found another bird, so they were not very quick on him and we soon lost him.

When we eventually stopped picking up, we had got forty-five of A's birds and failed to find thirteen. S. and I had got eleven and lost five. We had teal, wigeon, shoveller, and gadwall, so we were very sorry to have lost the pintail.

The dogs were much affected by the aster seeds, sneezing and having continually to stop and rub their eyes with their paws. The fuzz in their noses cannot have helped their scenting powers; but it was probably less tiresome than the strong smell of the aster flowers and the other rank vegetation had been earlier in the season.

After breakfast we were going out after snipe on the rest of the marsh, so decided to have another look for the lost birds. Besides my two Spaniels, I had with me a very old red setter, Ranger, who had spent the early morning in the car. He was an excellent snipe finder, and often very useful at marking dead game. When we began looking for the lost birds, he of course joined in the fun. Being fresh and having long legs he paddled about more than the spaniels and soon found a dead teal, which he marked. Then he stalked and snapped up a coot and so thought the whole show was great fun. After that he quickly found two more teal and a wigeon while the two spaniels between them only got one teal. Then he came to the downwind edge of a large pool and stood setting a clump of sedge which was in the middle of it. I told him to go out and he slid forward, like a cat, through the deepening water. On reaching the clump he took one slashing snap at it, then cocked one ear, with his head sideways, and returned to me. Knowing Ranger's habits I sent a spaniel to the clump, and there was a drake pintail with a neatly bitten neck. Ranger had done himself proud, perhaps not as a professional setter should do, but he added to our bag, which, after all, is the primary object of a gun dog.

In the subsequent walk round the marsh we accounted for a few snipe, a few more teal, and some game birds. Some of the snipe, a cock pheasant, and a woodcock would certainly have evaded us if we had not had Ranger to point them. This woodcock was resting in some long grass not far from the sea wall. He had probably only arrived the previous night, after crossing the North Sea.

Before midday we had finished shooting with a

total bag of ninety-one head, of which seventy-three were duck. This bag was made up of fifty-two teal, fifteen wigeon, four shovellers, one pintail, one gadwall, twelve snipe, one woodcock, two partridges, one pheasant, one coot, one moorhen.

CHAPTER IX

FRESH MARSH SHOOTING (*continued*)

It is sometimes possible to make quite a nice bit of duck shooting on ground which looks most unpromising. There are few places in the British Isles which do not have some resting place of ducks within four or five miles. On intensively farmed ground it is impossible to make a quiet stretch of sheltered water without considerable expense, but feeding places can be made very cheaply. A backwater of a stream, a wide dyke, or a cattle drinking pond is the only necessity, and this water need be of no great extent.

The whole art and secret of managing such a flighting pond consists of regular feeding every evening at the correct time. If the pond is near the house of someone who can see to the feeding, there is no great difficulty about its being done regularly. But, if the feeder has some way to go to reach the pond, it is sometimes extremely difficult to get the feeding done at the right time. ' Labour ' if left to itself is likely to do any job in the easiest way.

Feeding should be done just after sunset, and

the feed should be scattered round the pond and in the shallow water. If it is not scattered, the early arrivals or the tame decoys and the moorhens will get it all. If the feed is put down too early the same thing will occur. The aim and object should be to feed in such a way that any duck coming in during the night will find some food.

An inspection in the morning will reveal if all the food is gone, or if any is left. If much is left, then the ration should be reduced. If it is all gone, then increase the ration. But ducks are not the only things which will be attracted by the food. Moorhens and rats will certainly come, also coots if there are any in the neighbourhood. These should all be persistently persecuted. Every moorhen and coot in the territory over which the shooter has jurisdiction should be killed, if possible. Moorhens make excellent grouse pie and hare soup, also their wings supply feathers which are in great demand for making fishing flies; so the killing of them is not wasteful. Rats, of course, should be dealt with everywhere. The only way of catching them actually on the feed is by placing a trap under a box or in a hollow scooped under a wattle hurdle. Any other trap might catch a duck.

The feed used can be any kind of corn, acorns, potatoes, household scraps, cabbage leaves, and rabbit guts. Probably the best feeds of all are barley and rabbit guts.   Acorns have the great advantage that they are so large that the moor-hens cannot swallow them ; so, in a river back-water, they may be almost the best kind of feed.

The pond should be free from disturbance at night, but it does not matter what happens there in the daytime. If the pond is not on a flight line, steps must be taken to make the tame decoy ducks fly out to meet the wild ones. Sometime during the afternoon the tame ducks are driven out and prevented from coming back Then, if they are not too tame, they will go and settle elsewhere, possibly with other wild duck. At flight time they will return to the feed, perhaps bringing some of the wild ones from the pond on which they settled, or being viewed and joined by some other flighting ducks.

If such a pond is properly cared for, it will attract an increasing number of duck each year. The last ducks to come in should be allowed to do so undisturbed, thereby retaining the lead unbroken.

I am acquainted with a pond of less than thirty yards' diameter which has a large standpipe and chain pump in it, for filling water carts. It is, apparently, a much used and disturbed farm pond, yet it is a poor season when less than a hundred ducks are shot there. In this case the feeding

K

is done by a gamekeeper who understands his job and is keen on it.

The tame decoys which are kept on the pond should not be too tame, or they will not fly out to the wild ones; neither should they be too wild or they may not return at night. If they are too tame they can easily be made wilder, but the reverse is not true. A dog is a great help in driving out the tame ducks; one man with a dog being more use than a dozen men. If one man alone tries the job, the duck will settle on the fields when he is at the pond, and vice versa. If the man has a dog to attend to those which try to settle on the field, then he can give all his attention to throwing mud at the ones which settle on the water. This scaring of the ducks must not be done too suddenly, or there is risk of driving them out before they have learned to fly sufficiently well; in which case they may be too weary to return. It must always be remembered that the tame wild duck is the laziest bird in existence, if allowed to be.

If ducks are already using a pond, then it may be unnecessary to put down any tame decoys. Often duck come, in October, to any pond where there are oak trees, to eat the acorns. When the acorns are finished the duck cease coming. If feed is put down before the acorns are gone, the duck will continue coming. It may be thought that duck are using a pond, but no one may be able to watch it in the evenings. Under such circumstances, the best thing to do is to take a spruce branch or a broom or spade and smooth out all tracks in the mud of the pond, and if the mud is dry make it wet. An inspection early next morning will soon reveal the presence or absence of duck tracks. These ponds are usually used by pigeons, which come to drink in the daytime. They leave a lot of feathers about and so make it difficult to spot the duck feathers.

Most ponds can be improved by the planting of some weed which ducks like to eat, this making an added attraction.

Foxes are always a great menace to ducks, presumably because ducks have a much stronger smell than most birds. A raft moored in the pond and covered with either turf or gravel makes a fox-proof island on which the duck can take a peaceful nap and run little danger. If a raft is built, and boarded over, it should be tarred, and gravel thrown on to the wet tar. The rough surface of the gravel will serve to prevent mud or turf being washed off the raft. Quite a good temporary raft can be made of brushwood, faggoted and tied together. Empty oil drums make excellent floats, for raft building, and have the great advantage that they cost nothing.

If the pond is small the feed should be put at the upwind side only. The fox cannot then stalk by the use of his nose, but must use his eyes alone, which means that he must be visible to the ducks and so may be noticed when he moves. Also he may be smelt by the duck and the chance of his being heard is increased. Under perfectly natural conditions duck always prefer to feed and rest on the windward side of the water, and I believe this to be one of the reasons.

But if the pond is a very large one, the feeding place should be on the side which, with the prevailing wind, is down wind. The duck will then come low over the lee shore; whereas, if the feed is on the windward shore, they may come very high and not drop until they are over the water.

When choosing a position for the butt, from which it is hoped to shoot the duck, there are many things to be taken into consideration: the direction of the prevailing wind and of the sunset, the direction from which most duck will be coming and the form of the surrounding skyline. Endeavour to place the butt in such a position that the duck are at ideal range, say 20 to 25 yards, when they are to the west of the butt and so showing up against the brightest part of the evening sky. But this is often impossible owing to surrounding trees or the size and shape of the pond. Another good position for the butt is such that the ducks may be seen clearest when approaching. Of course, if the pond is large there must be a number of butts, but if it is small one or two butts is ample. One small pond, where I have sometimes shot duck, is in an open field with no trees to interfere with the shooter's vision. There are two butts, one on the south side, the other on the east side. The prevailing wind is from the south-west, so the duck usually approach from the north-east and are at perfect range from the east butt and showing well against the western sky just after they have passed the butt. If the shooter chooses the right moment to fire, under these conditions, the duck, as they leave the pond, pass to the west of the gun in the south butt and so give him a nice shot also. The one disadvantage of this place is that both guns have to shoot after the birds have passed them. On no account should butts on opposite sides of a small pond be occupied at the same time, as then neither gun is able to shoot at a low bird settling in the centre of the pond.

If there are many trees around the feed this may be the greatest controlling factor in the placing of the butts. There is a small pond completely surrounded by oak trees, whose heads form an almost complete canopy over it.

In October there are always some duck which come to this pond for the acorns. They come in high and drop almost vertically through a very small opening in the branches. Indeed, this opening is so small that I have often heard ducks collide in it. I found it quite impossible to shoot them as they came in, so devised the following plan. I placed my retriever on top of the bank of the pond on the far side from my hiding place, and, when the duck came I allowed them to settle undisturbed. I then whistled for the dog, thinking that the duck would rise the moment they saw him; but actually the duck delayed until the dog was already half-way round the pond; with the result that they flew out in such a way as to be invisible to me. The next time I placed the dog where he would show, against the sky to any bird on the water. The duck settled on the pond and almost immediately noticed the dog but were unable to decide what he was. After an appreciable space of time one suffered from broken nerves and led the party out in exactly the direction that I desired. The plan had worked.

Duck had visited this pond for years, in October, but it had never been thought worth while to feed there, and so keep them coming throughout the year, owing to the difficulty of shooting them. Now I intend trying to make it a permanent feed. Apart from the duck, it is a most amusing place to sit quietly in, on an October evening. The pond is on the side of a field which is surrounded by woods. The wood on one side slopes up to the crest of the hill, and near the crest grows a very old Scots pine, which is the roosting place of a family of herons. Close by it is an open piece of wood, overgrown with bracken and birch scrub, which is a favourite haunt of a small party of deer. As I have sat quietly waiting and watching the herons and rabbits I have heard the fallow buck on the hill roaring, or rather grunting, and being answered by a bigger one which lives in the wood on the other side of the field. I always hope to see these deer, but actually they never do come out in the open until it is dark.

Knowing that I must let the duck come in and settle, I am under no obligation to watch for their coming and can give all my attention to any of the other sights and sounds. So often, elsewhere, one is unable to appreciate the surroundings because of keeping all attention fixed on the watching for ducks.

The best duck shooting I have ever had has been on a marsh in the North of England. This marsh, or moss, is of considerable size, and consists of a flooded valley bottom which is almost flat. Stretches of open water are surrounded and interspersed with reed beds and sallow bushes. Surface feeding ducks can reach the bottom of most of the pools, except those in the centre, and they are of ideal depth for the diving ducks. The sea is close to one end of the moss, the two sides being closed in by wooded hills. A road runs round one side of the moss, and from this it is easy to watch the fowl, through telescope and field glasses, without disturbing them in the least.

On one occasion this year (1936) we stood on the road overlooking the moss. Teal were piping in the sedges close below us, beyond them were about fifty pintails, sleeping, preening, or feeding, as the desire took each individual; to either side of the pintail were wigeon, how many we could not see because they were in amongst the reed beds, but there must have been some hundreds. In the most open water in the centre were five male goosanders, with two females, showing bright salmon pink in the morning sunlight. Near them were about thirty tufted ducks and a pair of shellducks. In the reeds of the far side were a great many shovellers, the drakes looking very conspicuous, while the ducks were hard to see. Something disturbed the birds in the middle of the moss, and flock after flock of wigeon came flying down, some to settle near the goosanders, others to go on out to sea.

We got into our car and went to the far end of the moss. As we got out the telescope again, seven greylag geese came high over the hill, circled down, and settled amongst a mass of wigeon and coots in the centre of the open water. As the telescope traversed this line of birds, I saw the geese, the wigeon, the coots, then pochards, about fifty of them, some tufted ducks, more wigeon, seven golden-eye, and three goosanders. Away by themselves were a pair of red-breasted mergansers. In pools in the reeds were many swans, but the telescope showed all to be mute swans. We were disappointed in this, as there are usually some whoopers here, but the whole sight was one never to be forgotten. We had seen ten different kinds of ducks and yet were unable to see a single mallard.

Some years before, I had stood in the same place on this road and seen much the same scene ; but then I was unable even to think of being able to shoot on the place. But this day it was different, I was staying with a friend who had asked me to come and shoot there, and three days before we had shot it. A week before, the moss had been ice-bound, and the only birds on it were a very few in the pools of open water right out in the middle. The arranged shoot was almost cancelled, owing to this lack of fowl ; but, on the evening before, it began to rain and a soft wind blew, so it was decided to shoot after all.

As it began to get light we walked along the path which leads straight across the moss. Sometimes we walked and slithered on the hard ice, at other times we broke through and waded. Duck were flying about in quantities, but they were all passing over as there was nothing but ice. We could hear the greylags calling from near where I was to be placed, so it was decided that I should reach my place after the other guns were in position, as they might then get a shot at the geese which I was sure to disturb. As I was shown into my position, the geese got up and flew away, but they gave a chance to no one. I was shown where I could wade and where the water was too deep, then the keeper left me. I had with me as marker, J., and my dog, Poker, so I left them both in some sallow bushes. My position was chosen because a spring had caused a pool of open water amongst the ice. It was on this open water that the geese had been spending the night. The wind was blowing off my shore of the moss, so I waded out as far as I could and got down wind of the open pool, between it and the centre of the moss. The best cover was a patch of mixed osiers and reeds, and there I stood in about 18 inches of water. On my left the open water extended for 60 yards, but

all the rest of the way round me the ice edge
was just within shot. It seemed an ideal position
under the circumstances of frost.

Duck were coming in before I was in position,
so the fun started as soon as I was ready. I had
with me a belt containing thirty of a new brand
of cartridges, and some pockets full of my usual
cartridges. J. who was with the dog in the
sallow bush had my cartridge bag full of my
usual cartridges. I had decided to try the new
cartridges first and did so, and have seldom shot
worse and the less said about it the better. As
soon as I began using my usual cartridges I began
to kill the birds. I still wonder if it was the
cartridges, the improved light, or just my confidence. Those first thirty shots produced very
few birds. I could not tell their species in the
dusk, and the water was too cold to be worth
starting to work the dog, and the duck were
coming too thick. I know some of the birds
I missed were mallard. Later, when it got lighter
I could see that most of the birds were wigeon.
There were fewer teal than I had seen here on
former occasions. Some birds were passing
straight over or past, others came towards me
wishing to settle just behind me, others swung
in from the side to settle behind, then changed
their minds and came out low beside me. Most
of these last were shovellers, which offered easy

targets. There were very few large flocks on the move, nearly all the birds which came to me were in flocks of less than a dozen.

As it got light I could see my surroundings properly and was able to realize what an exceptional position I was in. The whole surface of the water was frozen, except for a pool in the most exposed part of the middle of the water. This pool was covered with coots and wigeon, in fact most of the wigeon which came in settled on this pool. Every now and then some of them would rise and try to come in to the open water where I stood. As I had no butt, and the osiers and reeds were not very thick, many of them saw me and turned off before coming within shot, but many others came admirably. At one time three wigeon came low to the left, looking for somewhere to settle. I waited for two to cross, got them with the first barrel and the other with the second barrel, then just had time to put in a third cartridge and get a teal which was coming high and fast down wind. The teal fell out on the ice and skated, spinning away like a curling stone. It was one of those little occasions which are remembered for a long time. Most of this morning was, for me, so full of incidents that I can remember few of them. Some which I can remember are: the one just related; the early morning missing of shot

after shot; a right and left of really high wigeon
followed as quickly as I could load by a right
and left of shoveller drakes; and another right
and left of wigeon which suddenly appeared
from nowhere; I first saw them, hanging in
the wind, almost overhead. I never saw them
coming and I do not believe they ever saw me.

When the main flight seemed to be over I had
down twenty-seven duck and a coot, but had
picked up none of them. There was only one
which I was afraid of losing, because most of
the other long shots had fallen on the ice and
never moved again, being killed by the fall.
I called up the dog, Poker, and went straight to
look for my doubtful bird, but could not find
a sign of it where I expected. However, Poker
found a dead bird close by, which, at the time,
I thought might be it, and am now certain was it.
We then waded round picking up what we could.
I worked the more open parts myself and kept
Poker working the cover. He found a wounded
bird and it dived, so I went to him and after
much waste of time we caught it. Of course it
was the coot. Then a single shoveller came over
and I brought it down winged and dispatched
Poker straight after it. Being a young dog, in
his first season, he did not know how to deal
with diving birds, so wasted much time on them.
I went to his assistance and fired five ineffective

shots at the swimming bird, then he caught it.
I was now clean out of cartridges so yelled to J.
to bring me the bag. While he was transferring
them to my pocket a teal came over and I got it.
Wonderful to relate, nothing had come within
shot while I had no ammunition. Poker, after
seeing me take the ducks away from him and
throw them on the heap which lay floating in the
osiers, thought he would save me trouble and
tried to take his birds to the heap and lay them
there himself. I tried not to let him do this, but
he actually did do it with a few birds.

When we had picked up nearly all that we
could get at easily, another movement of birds
started. I hurried into the thickest cover and
got another eight birds in as many minutes.
Then the keepers arrived. I had not let Poker
go on the ice because I did not know the depth
and formation of the bottom and I was afraid
that, if he fell through, I would be unable to
reach him. However one of the keepers managed
nearly to reach the ice edge and work his dog on
to it, when she got the eight or ten birds which
were there. On counting up my bag we found
we had picked thirty-seven ducks, and as I had
counted that I had thirty-seven down it meant
that we had not lost a single bird. In my experience
this is a very rare occurrence for duck shooting.
The bag contained twenty-three wigeon, seven

shovellers, four teal, one pintail, one pochard
and one tufted, also a pigeon and a coot.
Besides the six species of duck which I had shot,
I had missed mallard, golden-eye, and goosander.

This day was very different from another day
which I had on this same place one August.
The summer had been very dry and there were
acres of bare mud. The little water that was left
was almost unrecognizable, covered with floating
green brown slime that stank when stirred. The
heat was intense in the daytime, we wore an open
shirt and the lightest of coats, and at dusk there
were a million mosquitoes. Herons were
legion ; they rose squawking from behind reed
beds, flopped up and down the valley, and dropped
in great spirals, on stiff spread wings, from the
hard blue sky. Mallards were the most numerous
duck ; they flighted in for a drink in the late
evening and gave us great sport for the last ten
minutes of shooting light. The other ducks
were teal and shoveller, and we also got some
snipe and pigeons. None of these last were
flighting, but were disturbed by one gun and
flew over another. Although the date was only
the 10th August we did not shoot a single bird
that had not its primaries fully grown and hardened.
We lost a few birds owing to the rank vegetation
and stinking mud.

The place where I have had some of the best

early season shooting is a fen in Cambridgeshire.
Here there is a pool with reeds at one end and
surrounded by rough, rushy, grazing land. It is
right off the beaten track and is between no two
habitations, so that no one walks past it or
disturbs it. In the summer the fen is the breeding
ground of many snipe and redshank and a few
ducks the most notable of which is the garganey.
On the spring migration I have seen ruffs and
reeves, black-tailed godwit, and black terns, all
resting here for a few days and then passing on
to their breeding grounds. In winter there is
usually a hen harrier which hunts over the ground.

One morning in early August five of us met
at the end of the footpath which runs straight
down an old disused drove way for a mile or
more to the fen. It was very early and very dark,
but it was nice and cool. The previous days had
been scorchers. In single file we proceeded
down to the fen, the leader warning his followers
of the rabbit holes and other pitfalls in the path,
which would have caught the unwary. Before
we reached our destination we had decided that
we were going to be late, so hurried on as fast
as we could and arrived very hot and rather early.
We moved into our places, disturbing many
mallards, and had to wait some time before the
flight would start. My position was in a butt,
built of reeds, close to the water's edge. One

of the other guns was almost immediately opposite me, on the other side of the pool and about 70 yards away. The others were two at one end and one at the other.

As I sat on my shooting stick and waited, I got quite cold after the hot walk down. There was a nice breeze which would give a definite direction to the incoming ducks and might keep them down a bit ; but it did not affect the mosquitoes enough. They could easily hover about in the lee of the reed beds and inside the sheltered butts, so it was not long before they turned their attentions to the back of my neck and my wrists. Innumerable bats, attracted by the insects, wheeled and hovered and darted in all directions, the snapping of their jaws and rustling of their wings being one of the chief sounds of the place. At least one teal was flitting about calling with that note which is so difficult to locate. An owl, probably a barn owl, appeared so suddenly and silently that I almost shot at it, and then vanished as silently as it had come.

I wondered if any of the garganey would be shot. In one previous year there had been a most unfortunate slaughter of the innocents : five garganey being killed in mistake for teal. Then the rule had been instituted that no teal were to be shot at until the garganey had emigrated. Even then one or two were killed

L

in the first month or so. This day all of us should have been able to recognize garganey, so we hoped not to shoot any.

The first lot of duck came so unexpectedly and quietly as to find me quite unprepared. But my whistle put A. on the alert and the double splash which followed his shots told of a right and left which had opened the new season. The rest of the bunch went out over C. who missed them as they swung away in the wind. Shortly after this a quacking called my attention in the right direction and I got one out of five birds coming in low, my first barrel missing. I realized that I had shot at them in the wrong place, so that they turned away from all the other guns, instead of towards one of them. The shooting soon became general and each of us was getting shots either at birds coming straight in, or at birds which were going out again after being shot at by someone else. The best bit of team work happened when it was almost daylight. About thirty mallards circled round twice and settled in the middle of the pool, without anyone firing at them. My butt being on a promontory, it so happened that I was almost in the middle of the flock. When I fired they split up, and all five of us had reasonable shots at this one flock, getting seven of them. If any one of us had shot at them before, certainly

not more than two of us would have got
shots.

A few garganey came in and were safely
recognized, while the little flock of them, which
wheeled round from time to time, was quite
unmistakable in the daylight, to us who were
forewarned. There were fewer shovellers than
in other previous years. I shot a high one which
was a most satisfactory shot as it came straight
overhead. At the end of the flight we picked up
all we could, but left the systematic hunting of
the reed beds until later. On the way home to
breakfast we got a few snipe.

In the evening we went down early so as to
pick up the lost birds before the evening flight
started. In hunting out the reeds and bull-
rushes, I am sure that our dogs were hindered
by the smell of the rank vegetation. Also the
juvenile coots and moorhens, and one late brood
of ducks which were in the flapper stage still,
caused them and us many fruitless hunts.

The evening flight was not nearly so good as
the morning. The quantities of lapwings and
bats made it very difficult to spot the ducks. The
bats were in three sizes, of which the largest
had a very straight flight which made it more
duck like. There was no wind at all and the
mosquitoes were purgatory.

We ended the day with fifty-nine mallards and

five shovellers as well as some snipe and pigeons. Only two of these duck could possibly have been called flappers. One was a very young mallard caught by a dog and its neck wrung before its state was noticed. The other was an old shoveller drake, late in his eclipse moult, and with his primary feathers not yet fully grown.

Chapter X

THE PUNT GUN

Ever since I first began shooting I had always wanted to go punting, but not until I went up to Cambridge did I get the opportunity of doing so. There were, then, a great many ducks on the winter floods of the fenland rivers. We used to get a few by flighting them, and by sneaking about in an old Canadian canoe, but the main bulk of them we were unable to touch.

I bought a punt which, at the time, I thought was a good one, and borrowed an old muzzle-loading one pound gun. Neither I nor my friends had ever been punting, so we had everything to learn. I made innumerable mistakes in every possible direction, and got very few birds, but I learnt a lot of what not to do.

Later on, I was very fortunate in meeting an expert puntsman, while I was in Scotland. He took me out for a few days in his punt, and in later years we went punting together in many different places. Having previously tried and failed, I was now in a position to learn the right ways. It would be most tedious to chronicle all the mistakes, so I will only tell of the ways I found best, and the gear which proved most suitable.

For an outfit to be really efficient, the punt and gun must be properly 'balanced'. If a new outfit is being got, the first consideration is the gun, because it is the most expensive. Yet, perhaps, it is wrong to say that the gun is the first consideration, because the whole outfit has to be considered as a unit. On exposed estuaries and bays a double punt is almost essential. It can go with safety where a single punt dare not show its nose. On well sheltered waters, where only small lots of birds are encountered, a single punt is much preferable to a double. However sheltered is the fowling ground, a decked punt is always preferable to an undecked punt. It need be little or no heavier, is far less conspicuous and far more seaworthy. The narrower the punt is, the less buoyant it is and consequently the more of it is under water and the less conspicuous it is. But, it runs aground too soon, rolls about, and is heavy to push and very heavy to steer, if it is too narrow. If it is too wide and buoyant, too much of it is visible above water, and it becomes unmanageable in a wind. It is a fallacy to say that a single punt draws less water than a double, or that, because a single is smaller, it is less conspicuous.

The great advantages of double punts over

THE PUNT AS SEEN BY FOWL

[p. 166

singles are as follows: carry a bigger gun;
more seaworthy; when shooting, the gunner
has nothing to do besides aiming the gun;
after the shot there are two men to stop the
cripples; two is company. But there are many
fowling grounds where only small shots are
encountered. Here there is no need for a very
big gun, or for two cripple stoppers. The single-
handed fowler can go out whenever he wishes,
without having to get a companion, and so is
often quicker off the mark when fowl are sighted
from the shore. But the great drawback of
single punting is that the gunner does not have
both hands free for the gun. Aiming must be
done entirely with the punt, and consequently
he often dare not approach the fowl so closely
as with a double punt. Though the ' boot jack '
does enable the single man to elevate his gun
for a flying shot, he cannot do it with the same
nicety or aiming as the gunner of a double.

Roughly speaking, a gun firing over 1 lb of
shot is too large for a single punt. Any gun
can be mounted on a double, but it does not
seem worth while having a double to carry a
gun whose charge is less than 12 oz.

Even now, there are still people who are
prejudiced against breech-loading punt guns;
however, most fowlers are sure of the superiority
of breech-loaders. A muzzle-loader cannot be

cleaned so well as a breech-loader, and it is impossible to see down the barrel (unless the breech block is removed), consequently it is not so safe. The charge cannot be changed except with great trouble. The ignition is not so certain as with a breech-loader, though, with care, it is almost certain if the lock is good.

There are many different types of breech-loaders. Screw breeches are the best for large guns. In these, the breech block contains the striker and extractors, and has a male thread on the outside of almost its entire length. The breech of the gun barrel extends behind the chamber, and has a female thread to take the breech block. In some patterns the block is separate from the stock and lock, in others it is all in one piece. In the latter, before loading, it is most important to see that the gun is not cocked; as once the cartridge is in place inside the extractors, it can be fired by the striker. If this occurred when the breech was not screwed in, the resulting accident would almost certainly be fatal. I have a gun of this type and I always pull the trigger lanyard, as well as look at the dummy hammer, before commencing to load.

Another type of breech-loader has a sliding block, instead of a screw block, which is held in position by a block, pin, or pins, which rise up through holes in the breech part of the barrel and grooves in the block ; or else pass behind the block.

Another gun dispenses with the breech block, and has a vertical block which rises up behind the cartridge, passing through apertures in the top and bottom, and grooves in the sides of the breech. In this type the cartridges must be extracted with a special extractor, which is another bit of luggage to carry about. The snider action is also used for large guns.

For smaller guns, the above actions are used, but also the more ordinary breech mechanisms, such as a bolt action or sidelock, etc.

Above all avoid those breech-loaders which are intended to be ignited by a nipple and percussion cap as on a muzzle-loader. On the rare occasions when they do go ' bang ', the bang is preceded by the crack of the cap and the fizzle of the flame trying to get into the cartridge. Only the most unwary fowl wait for the climax of the fire-works.

If the would-be purchaser of a punt gun has no friend, who has experience of punt guns, to advise him, then let him go like Agag. Do not pay for a gun till you have tested it. I do not know of any London gunmaker who has any practical experience of punting, so they are not able to help a novice. My experiences, and those of my friends, when wishing to buy punt guns have not been entirely satisfactory. If I wished to purchase another punt gun I should demand a trial of it and I should have it in writing that I would refuse to pay for any breakages in event of the gun proving inefficient.

Repairs to these large guns, and new parts for them, are often most over priced. Where the ordinary gunmaker does not have tools and lathes large enough for working on big guns, if the owner knows, and can explain, exactly what he requires, he can often get the job done very well and reasonably by some firm of motor engineers in his neighbourhood.

There are various methods of taking the recoil of the big gun. The larger ones have either a breeching rope or recoil spring. Personally I prefer the rope for guns of all sizes. It is more simple than the spring. The boot-jack can be used on a small gun with or without a breeching rope. When used without a rope, the whole gun slides back underneath the fowler. Needless to say there must be no 'dog' on the hammer, or other protruding part on the gun, which might injure the shooter. If there is ice on the punt's floor, the gun may kick right back to the stern post! In the Cambridgeshire fens, some of the gunners have a wedge shaped block to take the recoil. The butt of the gun comes in contact with the vertical back of the wedge, while the gunner's chest is supported by the sloping front. In some cases this wedge is loose, and only held down by the gunner's weight. In other cases the wedge is fixed to the bottom of the punt. This is a very primitive method, as the gun can be neither traversed nor elevated. Most of these fenland fowling outfits are very primitive.

With a breeching rope, the strain of the recoil is taken by the stem-piece of the punt. In a properly built punt the stem piece is so fixed that really the strain becomes evenly distributed over the whole punt. The usual method is for the rope to pass through a hole in the stem, above the water line, and to come back along the top of the deck and be attached at each end to a trunnion on each side of the gun barrel. Sometimes the rope is led along under the decking, in order to keep it dry, the hole in the stem being inside the punt, instead of outside. The rope is more likely to rot when enclosed, and any wear and tear is not immediately visible, so it is preferable to have the rope outside. There are two disadvantages of the ordinary outside breeching rope; one that the rope shrinks when wet and stretches when dry; the other that the rope is one of the most visible things to the fowl, owing to the shadows cast by it and its getting blackened by the blast from the gun muzzle. How to counteract the former will be dealt with when the fixing of the gun is considered. The black appearance of the rope can be overcome by whitening it with ordinary whitening or pipeclay, a lump being kept on board for that purpose. It is very noticeable what a difference this makes to the 'camouflage' appearance of the punt. Painted ropes rot quicker than unpainted owing to the paint preventing their drying, so it is not advisable to use paint for this camouflaging. Manilla rope is the strongest and has the whitest appearance, but has most stretch and shrink. Tarred hemp has the least stretch and shrink, but looks almost black. If tarred hemp is used, one should specify " soft laid, tarred hemp bolt rope ". A soft laid rope is more resilient than a hard laid one, and so lessens the strain on the punt. If the rope breaks, the gun will hit the gunner, with most unpleasant results. Personal acquaintances of mine have been knocked out, had noses broken, and had teeth knocked in ; yet people still use inadequate ropes. Personally I use a rope that would moor a battleship, and get a new one every year. If someone else looks after your punting gear, cut up the old breeching rope. A friend of mine did not know that his man had put on the old rope, and he had a most unpleasant row home against the tide with his companion prostrate in the bottom of the boat and apparently lifeless. However, all ended well.

To fit a breeching rope, make a loop in one end large enough to slip easily on and off the trunnion, balance the gun in its correct position, put the loop on the trunnion and the other end through the stem, pull tight, bring the free end back and round the other trunnion, mark the exact place for the loop and bind it. Do not splice both loops, though you may splice one if you like, as the rope will stretch with use and you will want to alter the length of the loop. About a foot from the stem the two ropes will have to be tied to each other to keep them parallel up the deck, otherwise they would interfere with the elevator.

Some guns, instead of trunnions, have a ring on the bottom of the barrel, or a hole or 'horn' on the stock for the rope to pass through. The rope is then made fast to itself after passing through both the stem and the gun.

After loading, the gun must always be pulled back as hard as possible to ensure that the rope is taut. If this is not done, the gun will recoil so far that it will hit the gunner's face. It is advisable to pull back the gun before starting each stalk, especially when the rope is drying after being wet.

In a single punt, a boot-jack should be fitted as well as a rope. In this case the boot-jack is fitted entirely as an elevator, not with any idea of taking recoil. The gunner has one hand on the trigger lanyard, and one on the setting pole. He can traverse the gun by swinging the punt, but without the boot-jack he cannot elevate the gun. With the boot-jack he merely has to depress his chest to elevate the gun.

I prefer the balance of a gun to be such that a weight of 6 to 8 lb on the butt will elevate

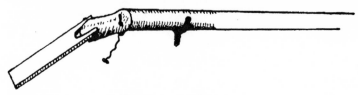

BOOT-JACK RECOIL

the barrel. If the gun is more evenly balanced, it will jump up and bang down in a choppy sea. If it is more muzzle heavy I find it difficult to hold on a steady aim. Having found the point of rest where the gun balances as described, mark it with a band of paint coloured differently from the rest of the gun. When this coloured band is resting on the gun crutch, the gun will be properly balanced, and a lot of tiresome trial and error will be saved by this visible mark, on each occasion that it is necessary to move the gun.

The gun crutch may be anything from an old
rowlock dropped into a hole in the gun beam,
to a beautiful gunmetal machine which can be
screwed backwards and forwards and up and
down, the screws being operated by wheels.
I have never had occasion to wish hurriedly to
elevate the butt end of the gun, and consequently
I consider these elevating wheels to be more
heavy and expensive than useful. But fore and
aft movement is essential, to counteract the

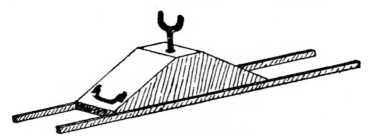

SLIDING GUN CRUTCH

stretch and shrink of the rope. This can be
attained by having a choice of three holes in
the gun beam, into which to drop the rowlock,
but this is rather a crude and inefficient method.

The simplest and best method I have seen, is one
whereby a block of wood slides fore and aft along
the floor, between two small wooden rails. The
crutch stands in a hole in this block. The fore
and aft movement is very easily attained by a
push or pull on the block. If required, the crutch
may be made to screw up and down in the block,

thus giving the means of elevating the whole gun. If a punt were being built, and this kind of crutch were decided on, it would be best to have the gun beam further forward than usual; as in this instance it does not support the gun but is merely needed as a strengthening for the punt. Whatever kind of crutch is chosen, it must be well padded. The best way of padding is to bind it with string and cover the string with leather.

In a well balanced gun the trunnions should be about a foot behind the point where the gun rests on the crutch. When a gun recoils it kicks straight back against the rope, stretching it very tight; the elasticity of the rope then throws the gun forward. If the crutch were too close to the trunnions it might be broken.

The muzzle end of the gun is supported by a rest, and it is this rest which enables the aim to be elevated correctly. The rest should be perfectly flat on the top. If the rest is crotched or notched, and the gun is correctly aligned when in the bottom of the notch, it is perfectly obvious that the barrel must be lifted out of the notch to be traversed to either side, and consequently must be aimed too high when shooting to either side. The weight of the gun barrel is enough to keep he gun in place without any notch. The rest which I use is a plain wooden ‘ bridge ’, the flat top covered with the worn tread off an old motor tyre and the feet covered with leather to make them slide noiselessly on the deck. The breeching ropes are inside the bridge, and a small rail on either side of the ropes prevents the rest from sliding sideways. The rest is pushed backwards and forwards by a long stick. An improvement on this, which I have used, is to have the little brass wheels off furniture castors put in a recess at the bottom of each foot; the rest then runs beautifully smoothly and silently, so long as the wheels are occasionally greased. The usual rest which is made like a plain bridge, is apt to be very conspicuous owing to the shadow cast by its forward side which is vertical. It is well worth making a sloping piece of wood to screw on the front of the rest, and so eliminate this shadow. The figure on p. 178 shows the plain rest and the one with a sloped front.

Personally I prefer to have the stick of the elevator on the right of the gun. The left hand is on the butt of the gun, to aim it, and the right can manage both rest handle and trigger lanyard. A shot should always be fired from the rest where possible. But when there is danger of running aground, the rest should not be used. Supposing the gun is on the rest and aimed correctly; immediately the punt runs aground up go the bows and the gun is aiming skywards.

M

Before the gun can be brought to bear on the birds again, the rest must be pushed forwards, and that takes valuable time during which many things are probably happening; the scraping

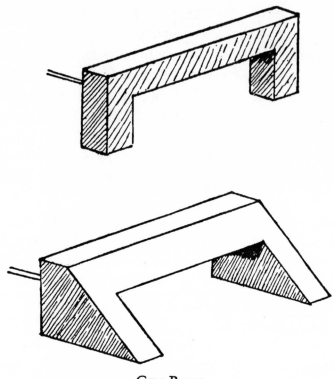

GUN RESTS

of the punt on the bottom has made the birds put their heads up, or they have noticed the sudden cessation of motion, or, worse still, the tide is swinging the stern round. I have seen many shots lost by the use of a rest. When punting in a fast tide it is almost true to say that the rest should not be used

When the puntsmen and gear are all in their right positions, lay the gun so as to bear on the water at 80 yards, now cut a notch on the under side of the rest stick where it crosses the edge of the gun beam. When it is so dark that the gun barrel cannot be seen, this notch can be felt to click against the gun beam when the gun is correctly laid. It is as well to make some other mark near the handle, which comes opposite some distinctive feature of the gun, as the rest running over a cockle shell or other foreign body will make a misleading click. But remember that a different puntsman, a number of dead birds, or just touching the ground will all throw the gun off its aim. It is far better to have a night sight of some kind. A strip of dull, black, insulation tape along the top of the barrel makes it fairly visible. If the foresight is a bead, get a black squash ball and make a small hole in it. This hole can be forced over the bead and will grip round the neck of it. If the ball is a new shiny one, sandpaper it to make it dull. But best of all, when it works, is a glimmer of light on the muzzle. Don't try phosphorous: when you drop it in the wet punt it jumps about with a series of explosions, and is a most unpleasant companion. Luminous paint is not bright

enough. The only thing is an electric light.
For this purpose a bulb holder is put on a clip
which fits the end of the barrel. The smallest
torch bulb is put in the holder, which is con-
nected by the requisite length of wire to a torch
battery and switch in the punt. Of course the
bulb holder is such that the light is only visible
from the breech end of the gun, and is the same
height from the barrel as is the foresight. The
bulb is then smothered with sealing wax to
such an extent that the light cannot be seen,
even in the dark. Now, with the point of a
penknife, or other instrument, scrape a small
hole in the sealing wax until the light is just
visible in a dark room. When the light is invisible in daylight, and just visible in the dark,
it is of the correct brilliancy. If it is bright
enough merely to be visible by daylight, it
will so dazzle the gunner that he cannot see
the birds by night. This ' light sight ' is admirable
when it works, but, unfortunately, electricity
and salt water do not agree. If the reader has
any practical knowledge of, and ability and
tools for, electricity and engineering, he will
very soon make himself a much better sight
than the one described. The little wooden
containers in which ' Hellesen ' bulbs are bought,
can be made into excellent bulb holders for the
light sight. They can be easily attached to one

of the metal clips which are used for holding tools on a workshop wall, and these clips are made in many different sizes, so that one can always be found to fit any barrel.

The best back sight for a big gun is a shallow V or notch filed in the trunnion band. Most fowlers do not pay nearly enough attention to the sighting of a big gun. Some merely point the gun in the required direction; others do not even do this, but have marks on their elevating gear, etc., and when all these marks are in the right position they say the gun shoots straight! This may be all very well for the owner of the gun, but it is not very helpful to the guest who is taken out for a day. Every owner of a gun should be able to say something like this : " At 60 yards the bead of the foresight should be in line with the birds and the neck of the foresight out of view, at 80 yards the neck and bead should be visible and the bead in line with the birds, at 100 yards the barrel at the base of the foresight should be visible and the bead in line with the birds." Of course, these instructions would be different in the case of different guns. A few shots at a vertical mud wall are not wasted shots, they will teach the gunner where the centre of his pattern goes. It is the correct placing of the centre of the pattern which leads to successful shots.

Since writing the above I have done various tests, with two different punt guns, at a target of sheet iron 10 feet long and 9 feet high. The resulting observations and suggestions are written down further on in this book. Amongst them is a description of a newly devised backsight.

The gun is cocked with a hammer or dummy hammer, the cocking piece of which should either contain a ring, through which a finger can be put, or be so large as to admit of at least three fingers or the heel of the palm being used when the hammer is being uncocked. One very cold finger cannot be trusted not to let the hammer slip. The firing is done with a trigger lanyard which should be knotted to prevent its slipping. Common knots rather offend my eye, and I like some fancy work in my trigger lanyard, but that is purely a matter of choice. I have found the following rule most helpful : " When the gun is cocked the lanyard must lie on the floor of the punt. When it is at half-cock the lanyard must lie over the stock." Thus the lanyard on the floor is a danger signal, and when wanting to fire it is necessary to hold the lanyard and if it is out of reach over the stock then it indicates that the gun is at half-cock and needs to be cocked. A still better plan is a peg, like a toggle, on the end of the lanyard, which goes into a hole in the stock when the gun is at half-cock.

Make sure that the half-cock is really safe. A gun belonging to a friend of mine went off and plastered a man and horse carting seaweed. Each of the punters blamed the other; one for leaving the gun cocked, the other for inadvertently cocking it. The gun was fired by pulling back the ammunition box against the trigger. Luckily neither man nor horse were any the worse for their dose of BB. About five years later I was out with the same gun. We were in a deepish, winding river mouth. The punt needed baling as we had just come round an exposed point where the sea was choppy. Leaving my companion to bale and clean, I walked upstream to see if there were any birds round the corner. Seeing no birds I began returning. At the water's edge there was mud, up the bank there was sand, so I came back along the bank. When I was within 50 yards of the punt, there was a sudden explosion, and the charge went up the water's edge beside me. Had it been sand at the water's edge, this book would not have been written by me. However, all was well. My companion was scared stiff, as he was unable to see me through the smoke for a few moments and so did not know whether he had got me. He then blamed me for leaving the

gun cocked, but I knew I had uncocked it.
The gun had again been fired by the ammunition
box hitting the trigger. We again put the gun
to half-cock and pulled the trigger, but could
not get it to go off. My companion was convinced that I had left the gun cocked. Then
I pulled the ammunition box along the floor,
so that it hit the trigger, and this time the

How to Carry a Heavy Gun

hammer fell. The unyielding jar of the hard
heavy box would fire it, but no amount of steady
pulling would do so. Obviously the gun was
to blame, we then said, and taking it to pieces
that evening we found that the half-bent of the
tumbler was broken. But it is possible to let a
hammer down to half-cock in such a way that
a jar will fire it. When a hammer is being let

down it should be let past the half-cock position,
the trigger released and the hammer brought
back to the half-cock position when the sear
engages with the half-bent. If the hammer is
let straight down into half-cock, the sear may

DOUBLE SHEET BEND

balance on the edge of the bent and in this case
a jar will fire the gun. I have seen old muzzle-
loaders with their 'innards' so rusted that it
is a mystery how the sear can find its way into
either bent.

A heavy gun is an awkward thing to carry.

The best way of carrying it, that I have yet found, is that which I have tried to depict in the accompanying sketch. Two pieces of rope are made into slings which go over the shoulder of the carriers. Because the weight of the gun draws the knot tight, it is as well to use a knot which can be easily undone ; such as the double sheet bend depicted.

When the weight is thus distributed between two arms and a shoulder, the gun is fairly easy to carry.

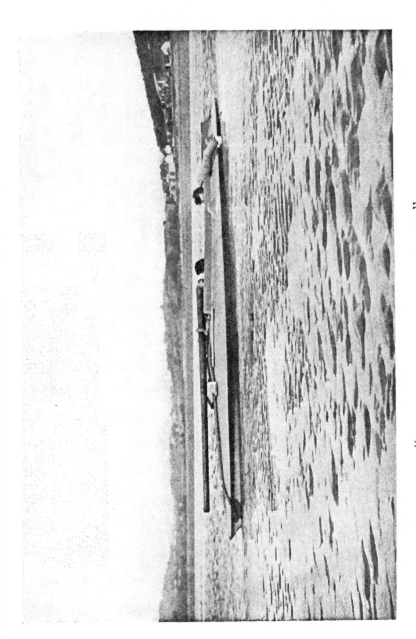

" BLACK HAIR SHOULD BE COVERED "

Chapter XI

THE GEAR FOR PUNT AND GUN

Now for the gear required by the gun; a ramrod and the ammunition box, which will hold the ammunition and cleaning gear, besides some cartridges for the cripple stoppers. The rod should be at least a foot longer than the gun barrel, to enable both hands to get a good grip of it in case the cleaner sticks at the muzzle end. One end of the rod has a brass fitting with a female thread to take a stiff wire brush and a jag. The wire brush must be brass, if it is steel it will rust to bits in the first ten days. Cotton waste is the best stuff to use on the jag. As to oil, personally I take a screw-stoppered beer bottle half full of motor engine oil. Unfortunately a screw stoppered square bottle is not procurable, so, to prevent the bottle from being able to roll out of reach under the fore-deck, I tie a piece of rope round it.

The ammunition box should be low enough to slide forward under the gun and be out of the way there. It has three compartments, one for big gun ammunition, one for cleaning gear, etc., and one for cripple stopper cartridges.

At least six big gun cartridges and sixty cripple-stoppers should be taken, or one day everything will go right, except that one runs out of ammunition. The cleaning gear, etc., will consist of cotton waste, rags, wire brush and jag, oil bottle, screw-driver, adjustable spanner, cleaning rod for twelve-bore, and twelve-bore cartridge extractor, also any special tool that the big gun may require. The adjustable spanner can be used as a hammer and with the screw-driver will do many useful jobs in the punt. A cleaning rod is sometimes needed to get mud out of the barrels of a cripple stopper. The best type is made by Messrs. Parker, of Birmingham, who call it the 'Helvetic' cleaning rod. It takes up little space, no parts can get lost, and it is assembled in about two seconds. Mud can be removed from a gun barrel by washing out in the sea, but remember to wash the extractors thoroughly with fresh water afterwards, then dry and oil. A drop down brass doorhandle may be fitted to one side of the ammunition box for ease in pulling it out from under the gun, and carrying it. The box and lid should be watertight. It will also make a good seat when rowing.

The cripple stopper cartridges should not be cheap non-waterproof ones, they are not economical for punting, as a good many get swollen and have to be thrown away. If the ammunition box is left in the punt between trips, a brass case cartridge is the only suitable one. Ordinarily, ' water-resisting ' cases are good enough. No. 7 shot is probably best for cripple stopping.

The punt gun cartridges need much consideration. For a small gun, brass cases may do, but steel are better. Unfortunately both brass and steel cases will expand after a few shots in a large gun, and so are not suitable. Paper cases are expensive to buy, and certain types cannot be bought. I believe that it is still possible to buy cases for Holland guns, and that they cost about eighteenpence each. On considering the time that it takes to make cases for oneself, it is really more economical to buy them at that price.

The following plan for making cartridges has proved excellent. The brass cartridge head is made as depicted. A is the base which has a male thread which screws into C, the washer B going between A and C. Up the centre of A is a hole which takes a blank revolver cartridge (6). A is shown with the dovetail (1) which fits in a groove in the face of my breech plate and is the means of extracting the cartridge. For guns which take a rimmed cartridge, of course this dovetail (1) will be absent. C is the lump of metal which carries the paper tube—C has an external diameter slightly less than A and B,

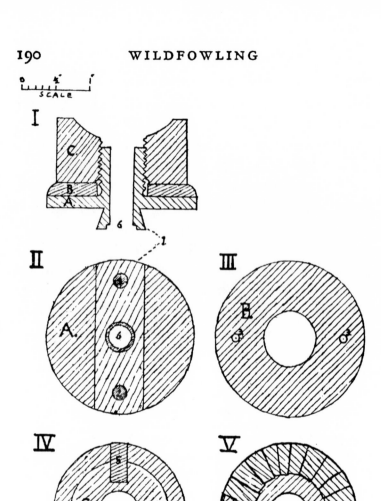

CONSTRUCTION OF CARTRIDGE FOR PUNT GUN

to allow for the thickness of the paper tube.
The two pins (4) fit into the holes (3) in the
washer *B*. The three pieces can be tightly

screwed together with the tools *D* and *E*. *D* is a flat piece of steel which fits into the grooves (5) in *C*. *D* must be long enough and narrow enough to fit down the paper tube. *E* has two steel pins which go into the holes (2) in *A*. A wooden roller *F*, is carefully made, of

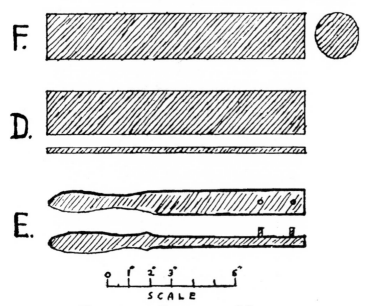

TOOLS FOR CARTRIDGE MAKING

hard wood, of such a size that the tube made round it will be of the correct dimensions. A piece of stout brown paper is cut in a rectangle whose whole length is sufficient to go from three to four times round the roller and whose breadth is a few inches more than the required length of the tube. The paper is now rolled round the

roller and stuck together with some paste, such
as 'Grip Fix'.   One end of the tube is now
trimmed evenly, if necessary, and C is put inside
it with the pins (4) pointing outwards. C is put
about $\frac{3}{8}$ in inside the tube and held firmly there
with one hand.   With the other hand a small
pair of scissors is used to make a series of straight
cuts all round the edge of the tube down to C,
as in Fig. V.   The little slips of paper so made
are now all bent inwards, overlapping each
other, the ones which would cover the two pins
are cut off, Fig. V.   The washer B is now fitted
over it, and A is screwed in, the whole being
tightened with D and E.   The blank revolver
cartridge is pushed into place in (6).   The cartridge
case is now finished and has the primer in it.
The powder I use is 'Colonel Peter Hawker's
Grain'.   If neither this nor 'Captain Latour's
Grain' is procurable, do not use a fine powder,
but use coarse blasting powder.   The ignition of
fine grain powder is much too quick; that of
blasting powder is only slightly slower than
proper punting powder.   For 'card' wads
I use linoleum and for 'felt' wads oakum.
Linoleum trimmings are easily got for the asking,
from most furnishers' shops.   Oakum should be
fine and tarry.   Sufficient should be used for the
wad to be longer than the width of the bore.
Having found the right quantity, weigh it and

measure it by that weight in future. It is impossible to measure oakum by eye, as some bits are compressed while others are fluffed out. The correct measure of powder is poured into the cartridge and a linoleum wad is pushed down on top of it. Now half the oakum is pushed down and rammed tight, then the other half of the oakum is also rammed tight. I find the best way of ramming is to have another piece of wood like the roller. After pushing in the oakum, I set the cartridge upside down on this rammer, hold the paper, and bump the rammer on a concrete or stone floor. By this means one does not crumple or tear the paper, and there is no possibility of hitting the cap as it is uppermost. The oakum wad should be firmly bedded against the powder, but there is a difference of opinion as to whether it, and consequently the powder, should be rammed hard or not. On top of the oakum is put another linoleum wad, then the shot, then a very thin linoleum wad which is gently pushed down on top of the shot. Now the paper case is trimmed down to the right length, which is about one-third of the diameter of the top wad above that wad. Now the tube is cut round in the same way as the other end was cut, and each slip bent inwards in the same way as in Fig. V. The end is now made fast with sealing wax, and the shot size

N

is marked, on the outside of the paper tube in large letters so as to be visible in the dusk. Then the paper part is given two or three thin coats of quick drying Shellac to make it waterproof. The cartridge is now finished (Fig. VI).

When a number of cartridges are being loaded, it is best to do all the powder first, then the wadding of each, then the shot. If different sizes of shot are being used, the cartridges are best marked before their shot sizes are forgotten. All gunpowder should be removed from near the bench before the sealing is done. I accidentally blew myself up with a pound of black powder at the early age of ten, and have not yet forgotten my lesson. I was not making punt cartridges, then, but 'mines' for the frightening of the household staff! Fortunately I received no lasting injuries; my shirt and hair were burnt off but both were soon renewed.

After each shot the gun barrel is best cleaned, and it *must* be cleaned if any of the old paper case is left in the barrel.

The loading of a muzzle-loader is very simple, if a little preparation is done before setting out. The powder is measured out and each charge is done up in a package of thin paper, the package being considerably narrower than the bore of the gun. Shot charges are wrapped in a similar way and marked with the shot size. The correct

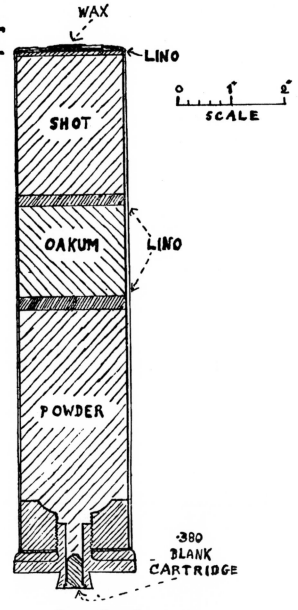

PUNT GUN CARTRIDGE

quantities of wadding are rolled into balls; large ones to go over the powder, small over the shot. To load the gun : a packet of powder is pushed as far as possible down the muzzle with a finger. A large ball of wadding is pushed on top of it, and pushed down with the ramrod and rammed as hard as possible at the end of the chamber. This ramming bursts the thin paper surrounding the powder, which is thus able to fill the chamber. The shot charge is then inserted at the muzzle, and a small ball of wadding after it. This is pushed up against the powder wadding with the ramrod. The shot charge and top wad are merely pushed, or tapped, and should not be rammed hard ; but they must be close up against the powder charge.

The only satisfactory ignition system for a muzzle-loader has a screw plug at the end of the nipple carrier. When the plug is removed, a needle can be pushed down the hole right into the chamber, to ensure that no obstruction lies between nipple and powder charge. Better than a needle, is a piece of copper wire ; it won't rust through and break off. Now the little chamber of the nipple holder is filled with powder of the same coarse grain as is used for the main charge, and the screw plug is screwed into place. The cap is put on the nipple and all is ready. If there are two nipples, so much the better.

The best way of dealing with the priming powder is to get a small oil-can of the type used for bicycles, and cut off the bit of spout which is too fine to let the powder pass through. This will hold more than enough powder for priming all the shots that can be fired in a day, and will keep it perfectly dry. The end of the spout will go easily into the priming chamber, and almost into the top of a nipple, so that, no matter how wet and windy is the weather, the priming is put into the gun perfectly dry. If the cap goes off, so will the gun which is loaded in this way. Caps are cheap and there is no excuse for putting them back in a waistcoat pocket at the end of the day. Once a cap has been put on the gun, if it is not fired, it should go overboard. The gun may be left loaded for a long time, but the priming should be changed every day. The hoarding of old caps and unwillingness to change priming saves the fowler a few pence and loses him many a shillingsworth of fowl.

The butt end of the ramrod should be brass, slightly smaller than the bore. This ramming end unscrews, revealing a screw for drawing the charge. A corkscrew on the end of the ramrod is better until it gets bent; unfortunately it always does get bent, as it is such a good flounder spear. A powder spoon is nothing but a nuisance and an extra bit of luggage.

It is best to clean out the gun after a shot and before reloading. For this purpose use a rag passed through a slot or hole at the other end of the rod.

To clean a muzzle-loader thoroughly at the end of the day, wash out with water as near boiling as possible. Some washing soda in the water is a good thing. Dry while the barrel is still hot from the water, and the heat of the barrel will finish its own drying. If the barrel can be removed from the stock, and the chamber end stood in a bucket of hot water, the cleaning rod will pump water in and out of the priming plug hole, and up and down the barrel, so washing it thoroughly. The best place to perform this is on a stairs ; the bucket being at the bottom, and the man cleaning the gun from the stairs. If the gun is being laid away at the end of the season, thoroughly wash out with changes of water, until the last lot comes away clean. Dry thoroughly and oil thoroughly, with any kind of medium oil. Put a plug of greasy tow in the muzzle, and an oily feather down the nipple, and you can safely leave it. Take the lock to pieces, clean, oil, and inspect it, and if any repairs are needed get them done now. Don't wait till the beginning of next season like I always do.

If you have no wire brush for the punt gun, a good cleaner can be made from a pot scourer ;

they are sold by most ironmongers, for cleaning out cooking utensils, and are made of metal shavings.

The gear required for the successful working of a punt cannot be acquired in a few minutes. A great deal of it must be specially made. The following is a list of the gear we usually carry:—

One pair of oars and rowlocks and a short-stemmed rowlock for sculling.

One mast, sail, etc.

An outfit of setting poles to suit the ground.

An anchor and rope.

A roller, or better still two rollers.

A baling tin.

A sponge or mop.

A pump.

The gun elevator and all the rest of the gear required by the gun.

Rowlocks must be specially made unless high unsightly blocks are used, as they must have high stalks. Galvanized iron is the best material, as gunmetal unfortunately arouses the predatory instincts of most beachcombers. The rowlocks are tied on in such a way that they can reach either rowlock hole or lie, under the side deck, on the punt's floor.

Oars should be light and strong. I prefer straight blades, as spoon blades are more noisy. A leather stop to prevent the oar sliding out of the rowlock is most useful at all times, but almost essential when cripple stopping in deep water. The ends of the blades must be copper bound, as they are sure to be used for occasional poling.

A sail in a gunning punt is only of use for running and reaching. The sail must be capable of being lowered very quickly when fowl are sighted unexpectedly. A high top is a disadvantage as it shows up for so far over the top of a sandbank. The fewer the spars the easier they are to stow.

A punt sail must always be a compromise between sailing efficiency and practicability. A jib-headed, triangular sail with luff laced to the mast and a loose foot on the boom, which is hinged on to the mast, is the most easily handled of all punt sails. The whole outfit is in one piece, and is set up and taken down by shipping and unshipping the mast. To stow the sail, the boom is folded up against the mast, and sail and sheet wound round the two. The two disadvantages are the length of the mast and the small sail area.

A spritsail has the disadvantage of a third spar. If it is of the usual, conventional shape, and it is bent to the mast, then mast and sprit combined make an awkward length for stowing. But if the sprit is attached to the mast within 6 inches of the boom, and is of such a length that the top does not come beyond the top of the mast, when folded, one gets a much bigger sail area than the leg of mutton and no longer has the disadvantage of the long sprit. If the sprit slips into a pocket at the head end, and is detachable from the mast, then it can be removed in a strong wind, thereby immediately lessening the sail area.

A lug sail is good for sailing, but a nuisance

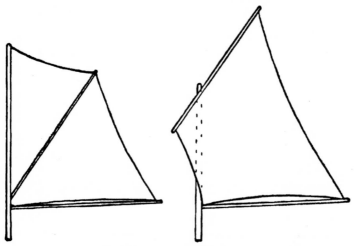

SPRITSAIL AND LUGSAIL

to handle. A gunter lug has the sole advantage of making long spars unnecessary; it is a brute to handle in a hurry and the jaws of the boom and sprit are always in the way when stowing. For a lug for a punt, the yard should not be too upright, because with a well-sloped yard a boom is unnecessary. The tack should have a loop to go on to a hook on the mast. The halyard is used as a shroud and taken down to a ring or cleat on the deck on the weather side. The lack of a boom is only felt on a dead run, with this sail, and on such occasions a setting pole can easily be used to hold out the foot.

The sketch shows the method of attaching the sprit and boom to the mast, for a spritsail.

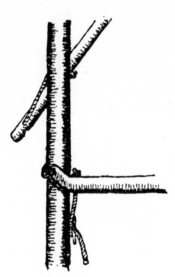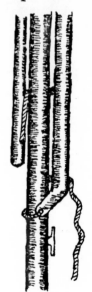

SPARS FOR SPRITSAIL

The sprit has a hole through its lower end and the mast has a hole, running fore and aft, through it. A heel rope passes through both holes and has a knot at each end to prevent its slipping out. This heel rope must be long enough to allow the sprit to pass right round the mast. If it is not long enough, and for any reason the sheet is let go when the sprit is round the mast, then something must break unless the mast turns round.

The boom has jaws set on at an angle of 135°, and a rope passing from the end of one jaw to the end of the other. This rope prevents the jaws from coming away from the mast. The jaws are set on at an angle of 135° because that best enables the boom to fold up against the mast, without reducing its strength or efficiency. There is a heel rope for tightening or slackening the luff of the sail, according to whether it is wet or dry. On the mast is a cleat for attaching this heel rope.

The sail should be laced to the mast and be loose-footed. The sprit can go into a pocket at the top of the sail, or be attached in the more usual way. The mast head should have a shroud attached to it; this need not be used unless required.

A sail of this type can be taken down as quickly as any other type of sail. If the shroud is not being used, all that need be done is to take the boom and sprit up to the mast and lift the whole out of the mast fittings. The sail is rolled round the spars, and the sheet round the whole lot to keep them together for stowing under the fore-deck.

Whatever sail is used, the mast will be stepped

in a block on the punt's floor (not floorboards) and held upright by passing through a ring bolt in the gun beam.

In a light wind this will be sufficient, but a single shroud is often necessary. With a lug sail this will be the same rope as the halyard. With a sail bent to the mast, a loose shroud should be permanently attached to the mast head. A square foot to the mast, fitting into a square hole in the floor block, is unnecessary and soon wears off. A round foot and round hole are much to be preferred, as it does not matter in the least if the mast does turn round. The mast should be thickest at the part which rests in the ring bolt, as the greatest strain comes here.

An ornamental truck is only a nuisance: the mast head should merely be rounded. The ends of all other spars should also be rounded to prevent their tearing the sail. The sail should be of very light material, ordinary canvas is too heavy to roll up into the small space essential for stowing. The sheet can be quite light, but if it is much thinner than an ordinary lead pencil it cuts into the hand which holds it.

The floor block for holding the foot of the mast must be attached to two cross timbers as well as the floor. The cleats for the shroud or halyard should be bolted through the deck and into a small block of wood. They should be placed, one on each side of the deck, where they are most out of the way and take the direct strain with a wind on the quarter. They will then take a good deal of strain when either running or reaching.

The insignificant looking setting poles are some of the most important of the puntsman's outfit, and need careful making. One sees many setting poles so clumsily made as to be almost useless. A perfect setting pole must be correctly weighted and balanced, have a good grip for the hand, be nicely stream-lined and well shod. It is best described by the diagram.

The handle of the pole should be small, with an oval section, but the edges of the oval must not be in the least sharp. The grip cannot be too smooth. A rough grip soon blisters a wet hand. The knob on the end should be more or less the shape of the handle of a Canadian canoe paddle. It serves two purposes; one for preventing the pole from slipping the grasp when setting to fowl; the other for a grip for the upper hand when cruising along. A section of the 'blade' of the pole should be a sharp-edged, narrow, oval. The iron shoe should be of such a weight that the finished pole sinks to the bottom and stands upright. Many fowlers prefer that the pole should float in an upright position; but

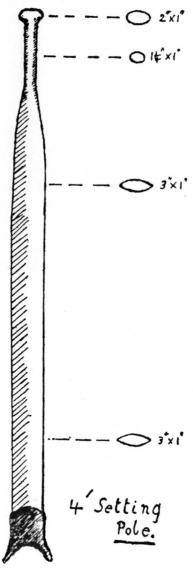

4' Setting Pole.

SETTING POLE

it will be found that such a pole requires to be pushed down and so is not so efficient for its purpose of setting to fowl. The shoe is easily made by a blacksmith. The wooden blade is inserted in the shoe and riveted through. The prongs should be about 2 inches long and rounded at the points. Sharp points tear sails and puncture boots.

The type of shoe just described is far the best for general purposes and perfect for sand ; but it is noisy on stones and sinks into mud. The former is easily overcome by having a pole with no shoe, wrapping the requisite weight of sheet lead round the foot and fastening with copper tacks. This is beautifully silent, but has the disadvantage of slipping. The sinking into mud is not so easily overcome. If anything is put on the pole to deter it from sinking in it usually prevents it from pulling out.

The best anchor for mud and sand is a stockless anchor, as it lies flat on the after deck when not in use. Unfortunately it is a very bad type of anchor on stones. The best all-round type is a grapnel with good wide flukes set back from the points. This will dig well into sand or mud, and usually finds a crack in stones where it can get a hold. Its only disadvantage is that, when stowed, one of its arms is always sticking up in the air. An anchor with folding stock is not advisable, as the stock has a habit of folding up and letting the anchor drag when it is most wanted to hold. But a folding grapnel is excellent if treated properly. ' When folded it lies flat, and when unfolded it cannot fold itself up. The one danger is that a novice may heave it over without unfolding it, and the owner may fail to notice what has been done.

The anchor rope should be as light as is consistent with its safety; a heavy rope does not coil down so neatly in a small space. The rope is attached to the punt by means of a shackle bolted through the stern post. The best way of attaching this rope to both the shackle and the anchor, is by means of a round turn and two half-hitches and stopping the end back (*i.e.* lashing the end to the standing part of the rope).

About 30 feet of anchor rope is required. One seldom wishes to anchor in more than 12 feet of water. An anchor chain is not advisable as it is so noisy. The rope must be frequently inspected. A breakage might be fatal to the puntsman.

Occasionally it is necessary to anchor and lie waiting for fowl to come into a position favourable for a shot. On such occasions it is essential to be able to take up the anchor without getting up from a lying position. Eighteen inches or 2 feet of rope with a hook at either end is invaluable at such times. One hook is put through a

ANCHOR ROPE AND STERN SHACKLE

ring under the side deck while the anchor rope is passed through the other. The punt is thus no longer anchored from the stern but from the side, within easy reach of the punter when he is lying down. When the anchor is not in use, it lies on top of the coiled anchor rope on the stern decking. In a sea and when sailing it should always be brought inboard as it may cause an accident if it inadvertently falls overboard.

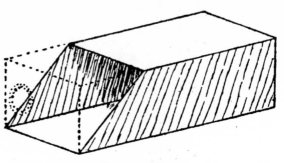

BALING CAN

The rollers are only wanted occasionally and so, if taken, are stowed well forward under the fore-deck. They are used for rolling the punt over hard ground and as levers for lifting the ends round, etc. Three inch diameter is a good size. The mast can be used as one roller.

An excellent baling tin is made from a 5 lb Curtis and Harvey powder tin. This being flat, suits best in a flat-bottomed boat. After cutting the tin as shown, the edges should be turned in to avoid their cutting anything. If a pump is used, the floor boards need not be taken up as it can be operated through holes in the floor boards. But a pump is very slow in dealing with a lot of water and never gets the last drop. A sponge or mop is essential for cleaning up punt, boots, etc. If the sponge is sewn up in a piece of cloth it lasts very much longer, or numerous bits of sponge can thus be converted into one sizable one. The sponge is best kept in the baling can, under the stern deck.

A leather baler as described by Sir Ralph Payne-Gallwey should be excellent, but I have never tried one. Its apparent advantages are noiselessness and flexibility.

Chapter XII

PUNTING

The arrangement, ordering, and working of a day's punting are best described by depicting an actual day: not a theoretical day, but one which really occurred. In my experience there is no such thing as a typical day's punting; each day has at least one feature which sets it apart from all others. I think this is why the theoretical days described in most wildfowling books do not ring true, and consequently give little real interest to the reader.

This day took place in the last week of October. A narrow burn, running out across the sand into the mouth of a very large estuary, forms the background of the story. There is no wigeon grass or other feed on the sand, so it is merely the resting place of the fowl which go elsewhere to feed. High water was some two hours before dawn, and there had been a lot of rain so that the burn was in spate.

Our plan was to try for a shot at the greylags when they came to wash at the first light of dawn, so 5.30 saw us started down on the ebb tide. Everything was in its place in the punt. Right

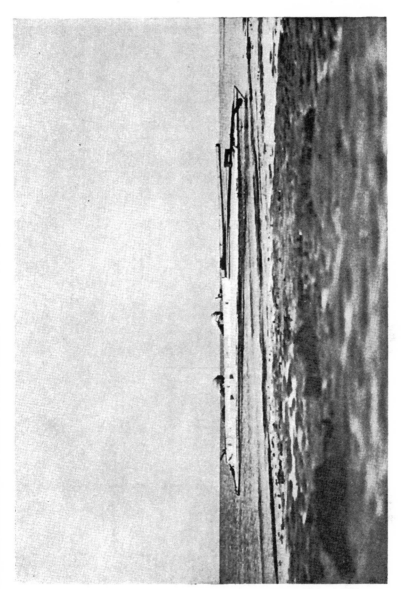

"LACK OF SHADOW TENDS TO HIDE THE PUNT"

[*p*. 212

forward under the fore-deck were two rollers. On one side, also under the fore-deck, the mast and sail and two cripple stoppers ; on the other side a pair of oars and the cleaning rod for the big gun. Under the gun and up against the gun beam is the ammunition box. Under the side decks are a large thermos flask and the gunners' field glasses. On the shelf under the stern seat are the punters' glasses and some sandwiches. It is a wet morning of rain and mist so we are wearing our oilskins : had it been fine, these would have been used to lie on, or stowed under the side decking. H. was the punter and I was the gunner.

For the first half-mile the wind will be on the right of the punt, so H. lies on the left and uses his left hand while I lie on the right. The water will nowhere be very deep, in some places very shallow, so the longest setting pole is left on shore. In H's hand is a 3 ft setting pole, beside him is a short 18 in pole and in front of him, on the deck, is a pole of about 6 feet. On my left are the other poles which are not wanted at the moment ; an 8 ft pole and a 4 ft pole with no iron on its head, only lead, also another 18 in pole for the use of the gunner in case of difficulties.

On first entering the punt, the gun was inspected to see that the barrel was clear, loaded, and then pulled hard back on the breeching ropes to ensure that they were taut. Now that we are actually ' going into action ' and likely to meet the geese at any moment, as the previous high tide may have drifted them right up the burn, we must be prepared for a shot. It is still what a landsman would call ' dark '. If geese could be seen with the naked eye they would be within shot. I confine my whole attention to looking through my field glasses. The rain is very much of a nuisance, as the glasses soon get misted over. The novice finds very great difficulty in identifying the species of birds under these circumstances ; they are unseen one moment and the next they appear, looking colossal and more or less shapeless. After a little practice the smaller gulls, curlews, and oyster-catchers cease giving over-anxious moments, as they were recognized at once. But the big black backs and mergansers are always hard to identify in the dark.

Our first few hundred yards take us through a flock of oyster-catchers, some scattered curlews, and a great many gulls. We are fortunate in passing through the oyster-catchers, as, so often, they are apt to fly twittering along in front of the punt. Suddenly there is a noise of geese close in front of us, which is answered by others out on the sand to our right front. A few seconds later the ones in front are visible ; five of them scattered about on the right bank. Then they can be seen with the naked eye and the gun is brought to bear. H., with great skill, keeps the gun 'on' them and we quickly drift up to and past them, but we are never able to shoot more than two, so do not fire. As we came abreast of them they saw us, but did not rise till we were almost out of shot beyond them. Sometimes when geese see a punt they run together and offer a nice shot, but these did not do so. However, from when they were first seen to when they got up the gun was aiming at them, though in the end we were retreating stern first. A manœuvre like this, in a fast current, is a lot easier to describe than to perform.

Another hundred yards and we were past the places where we had hoped for a shot at the greylags. Now we must wait for a better light, as there might be ducks below us. Another possibility was the bernacle geese which often come, just before sunrise, to wash in the stretch below us. As we lie waiting for the light to improve, the mallards come out from the land and fly on down the burn, the gulls and curlews and some of the geese go the other way, into the fields to feed. Then about fifteen greylags fly down to the channel edge some way below us. In a moment we are starting for them. When we are still a long way from them we hear the yapping of a pack of bernacles. These soon come in sight heading straight towards us up the channel, which is quite wide in this stretch. To be or not to be? Will they settle in front of us, or will they give us a flying shot? There are about a hundred of them. There is a steep, cut edge to the sand on our left; the stream has cut it away, leaving a vertical wall about 3 feet high. We are tight up against this wall and so almost invisible. On come the bernacles straight up the channel, looking, head on, like gigantic driven grouse. The current is very strong, making it impossible to aim the gun anywhere except down stream. Here we are looking across their line and so they are not worth a shot. As they pass us they suddenly wheel and cross our stern, presenting a mark like a barn door. If only we had been facing the other way! These bernacles now go right away and out of sight.

The greylags are still at the channel's edge and now we are nearer. They are on the left of the channel, the same side as we are. But where they are the sand has little slope and so the water is very shallow, the main force of the stream going under the right bank where it has formed another cut edge. We follow down the main run of water, travelling very fast, and cross to the other side about 250 yards from the geese,

which, fortunately, do not spot us. At 120 yards
we turn across the stream and head for the
geese. As the punt leaves the run, the bows
come into slacker water while the stern is still
in the run, and, for an instant, the punt goes
almost broadside to the geese. At once they see
it and telescope their necks. A mighty push
swings the punt back again and once more the
gun bears on the birds, which are still hesitating.
While they hesitate the punt almost leaps forward,
from a hundred yards to eighty. The first one
stretches his wings and the gunner fires. The
shot catches them about 6 feet up in the air, then
all is obliterated by the smoke. We both get
to our knees ; H. pushing hard towards the dead
birds and keeping his eye on the flying ones,
while I pull out a cripple stopper and load it
and put some cartridges in my pocket. One bird
is running away across the sand while the four
others all appear dead. I jump ashore and soon
shoot the cripple and then collect the other four
geese. Meanwhile H. had marked a dropper from
those which flew away. It lies a third of a mile
away on the sand, apparently dead, on the right
of the channel.

Suddenly the 'Hoop, hoop, hoop a hoop'
of wild swans is heard, and seven of them come
across from the west and settle on the sand
not far from the dead goose. There are four

old white ones and three young dirty coloured ones. A few seconds are spent in singing, then all seven go straight to sleep without even preening their feathers.

I set out for the dropper while H. cleans and reloads the big gun, then stows the geese and sponges up the few traces of blood, sand, and water. I take with me my glasses and gun and a setting pole. The goose appears dead, but then so have others in the past, hence the gun. The setting pole is useful in wading across creeks or going near quicksands.

The whoopers are so tired that they allow an approach as close as 200 yards, when they get up and only fly about half a mile further out on the sand. The goose is dead, having been shot in the lungs. On my returning to the punt, all is in order again and we have a cup of hot coffee and some sandwiches.

From this place the next mile of channel appears empty of fowl. As there is so much fresh water in the burn it will be possible to return now without waiting for the tide to flow. We decide to do this.

When about half the distance has been covered, we notice a small bunch of geese, only about half a dozen, still sitting on a stony bank higher up the burn, near the place where we saw the five in the dark, but on the opposite bank.

The oars are quickly stowed away again, and
once more we are lying down. The greylags are
sitting on the outside of a bend of the burn,
where it is very narrow. The whole punt will
be almost hidden by the bank until within 120
yards, after that it will be in full view but its
course will be straight for the geese. But this
last 120 yards will be on the stony ground
where an iron shod pole would make a great
deal of noise, so the lead ended pole is put in
readiness.

The first, and easy, part goes according to
plan. As we reach the beginning of the bend,
H. brings his iron shod pole in board and takes
the leaded one, effecting the change with scarcely
a sound. There is still some more sandy bottom,
before reaching the stones, and the pole slips
abominably, reducing the speed of the punt
just where we want to increase it. One of the
geese sees something suspicious and has a good
look at us, then seems to think that everything
is all right after all and concentrates his attention
in the opposite direction. About a dozen or
fifteen more geese suddenly appear flying out
from the land. They see the ones in front of us,
which are now almost within a long shot, and
glide in to join them. Our birds give all their
attention to the new comers, and we are closing
in at a good speed. The sight of these geese

gliding straight at us, then dropping their legs, throwing up their breasts, and backing with their wings as they pitch amongst the others is quite unforgettable. Every little black spot on their breasts is visible to us, they appear so close. However, they have hardly settled before they see the punt, but it is too late and the shot takes them as they rise. Again six are killed, all stone dead this time as we were so close to them.

In a very short time we are back at the mooring place. The time is eleven o'clock, and we have already had a good day, though we still have the prospect of another shot in the evening, when the water will be high at the time that the geese come out from the land.

It certainly was not a typical day, for we did not even lie down preparatory to stalking any ducks, as there were no ducks worth stalking. Also we had one shot at the geese in broad daylight and another when it was almost daylight.

Usually the only good chances at geese are those which occur in the dawn or dusk, but the best chance I ever had was in brilliant sunshine in the middle of the day. We had already had two stalks at wigeon and mallard, but they were very wild indeed, owing to the brilliant sunshine. We were punting from my motor-boat, so when we reached the end of one channel we cruised off to another one some two miles away. The weather was so calm and the sun so hot that we took off our coats and lay on the cabin top basking in the heat. As we passed the light-ship we saw the pilots also enjoying the warm weather and hanging out all their washing. Four or five shrimpers were trawling in the mouth of our channel.

As we drew in sight, we could see two or three bunches of geese not far from the water's edge and some more high up on the sand.

Further up the channel were thousands of wigeon, all very scattered and in the water; while nearer to us was a large flock of knots.

One day in the previous year, late in the season like this day, I had found all ducks unapproach-ably wild yet I had got a shot at the pinkfoots. The remembrance of that encouraged me to try for the geese. We motored on past the trawlers and looked at the geese from a different angle. As we watched them one gaggle flew down almost to the water's edge. Immediately we prepared for action. D. and I got into the punt; he at the the gun, I to do the punting. We lay down and were towed up the channel by the motor boat. We went past the geese and up to the wigeon, which flew out to sea at our approach. Then the motor-boat turned in for the shore and slipped our tow rope and turned off again when I signalled that I had the bottom with my setting pole. As we started the stalk, she went back to cruise about in the channel opposite the geese, to try and distract their attention from us.

The wind was from our left, which was the shore side, so I had to push with my right hand and rely on D. to tell me of any points jutting out from the shore. The first part of the stalk was along a shore which I knew well, then there was a big wide creek and then a very flat shore which I had never stalked down before.

Twelve geese flew across from the other side of the channel and settled between us and the thirty or forty which were our objective. They started to swim towards the others directly they had settled. We decided to give them time to reach the others.

The first part of the stalk went well and without incident. As we neared the creek I got the punt moving as fast as I could, so as to get enough way to carry us over the deep water where I knew that I would lose the bottom. We cleared the creek all right and then started down the shore, going slowly so as to let the twelve geese join the others and also so as to reserve my energy for the last rush.

The twelve geese swam slowly on in front of us and I noticed that they were not pinkfoots.

They had the carriage of whooper swans; long body and long straight neck with head set on at right angles. I felt sure they were bean geese, but said nothing to D. for fear of disappointment. The bean goose is our rarest goose and neither of us had ever shot one.

Apparently D. was also thinking the same thing and, with all eyes on the birds, failed to notice an outjutting spit of sand. We went hard aground and got off with difficulty. After rounding the sandspit I went straight for the end of another spit and suddenly lost bottom between the two. This delayed us a long time, but as it was almost calm and the tide was almost dead low I paddled across with the short pole instead of risking the noise of changing poles.

Why neither the running aground nor my losing the bottom was noticed by the geese, I still do not know. Just as I got the bottom again, a small gaggle got up from the high sand, flew over another big lot of geese and settled in the water's edge. The big lot followed them and also settled and the ones we had been stalking walked down and joined them. The bean geese were still swimming towards them and only about sixty yards from them. We, in the punt, were almost within shot of the bean geese.

I put every ounce of energy behind my shoves, and as the bean geese joined the others we came within a long shot. The edge of the shore and the shallow water was like Brighton beach on a bank holiday. Each bird was intent on bathing or greeting its neighbour. The punt was going well straight for the birds which stretched in a long line straight away from us. Suddenly all was silent, a forest of necks sprang up and, for an instant, all eyes were on us. Then with a mighty clamour they jumped up and the gun went off. The smoke prevented me from seeing. I knew the shot was too late but I hoped the gun had been elevated to counteract the lateness. The people in the motor-boat saw exactly what had happened and saw the birds drop from the bottom edge of the flock.

When the smoke disappeared I was bitterly disappointed. It had been the one chance of a lifetime. We had a long cripple hunt, because it was only the outside of the pattern which had hit the birds, so few were killed dead. When we had got them all, we had ten pinkfoots and four beans.

How often does ' the one chance of a lifetime ' fail to come off? I can think of a great many times when it has failed and not once when it has succeeded.

There is a bay where many wigeon spend the winter. The whole of this bay, except one small river mouth, is exposed to a certain wind. When the wind blows strongly from this direction, all the normal resting places of the wigeon become a sea of breaking waves, and they go for shelter in the river mouth. On such a day H. and I saw dense masses of fowl resting on the banks of this river. We hoped that the storm would continue, put the punt on the trailer and got all ready for the morrow. When dawn broke we were launching the punt where a road runs down to the river. The torrents of rain which had fallen during the past two days, added to the ebb of a spring tide, caused the river to flow with great force. We waited for the light to become good and for the tide to ebb a little further, then we started down stream. Between the high, wall like banks we travelled at great speed; sitting up and rowing as there was no chance of a shot for the first three-quarters of a mile. Then, leaving the rowlocks in position and oars lying ready on the side deck, we lay down to round the first corner. There was nothing there. Hurriedly sitting up we rowed across the river to get on the opposite bank and so come round the inside of the next corner. So strong was the current that we only just had time to lie down again before being swept round the bend. The heads of five wigeon showed over the bank, and the next moment we were almost on top of them. They got up and flew

P

round the next bend dropping straight down and settling. From their way of doing this we knew that they must have seen other wigeon and joined them. Another hurried pull across the channel brought us on to the inside bend. As we lay down again we heard the noise of many wigeon and knew they were sitting just round the corner.

We swept round and into the straight stretch as though we were finishing a fast race. More than a thousand wigeon were on the bank and in the water's edge, stretching straight away from us. We were going so fast that we were within 30 yards of the nearest birds before a single head went up. I aimed the gun so as to hit those nearest birds with the bottom of the pattern, knowing that there was 80 yards of wigeon, packed like jam in a pot, stretching away beyond them. As the first head went up I pulled the trigger string. 'Click': the gun had misfired. H. swore violently. I was too busy to swear. Reaching forward I re-cocked the gun and in so doing altered the aim. Crashing the gun back on to the last remaining birds I pulled again and this time it went off. But very few birds were left by then.

We got out the oars and pulled straight past the cripples. Then when we were below them all I got out a cripple stopper and dealt with each one as it was swept down past us by the current. Picking up the dead ones in the water took some time and we ended up nearly half a mile below where we had had the shot.

Then leaving H. to pole slowly up the side of the current I walked up one bank, looking carefully in all the gutters, for we knew that some cripples had sought shelter on this bank. Only one got back into the water and I knew I could leave that to H. When I had searched every little hidy-hole I returned to the punt and crossed over to search the other bank in the same way. We picked up twenty-six wigeon, which would have been a very good shot in the ordinary way, but had the gun not misfired at the first attempt we should have had a shot to go down in the annals of wildfowling history.

It is not always the biggest shots which are the most successful ending to a stalk. Sometimes I have had a shot of seven or eight birds which was the most that could be hoped for. Of course, it is not a good thing to have a shot at a big lot of birds, merely for the sake of getting a few. It is much better to leave the big lot undisturbed until the day comes when they are rightly placed for a big shot. But there is no harm in having a go at a small bunch of birds, for the sake of a small shot.

On one occasion I took out a friend M., whom

I especially wanted to have a decent shot. Birds were not plentiful and the weather was so calm that what few there were were sitting out on the deep water. The only chance we saw was a small bunch of nine wigeon. As there was nothing else to do I said we might push up to them and see what they looked like when we got close to them. As we neared them they appeared all bunched together, except one which was a little to one side. The stalk was easy, nothing went wrong, and M. killed all the eight stone dead.

But the smaller the bunch of birds the easier they are to stalk, so a small shot is not such an indication of skill as a large shot. Actually the best shot I have ever made at wigeon called for extremely little skill on my part. It happened as follows.

P. had had the punt out on the previous day, come up on the high tide in the dark and left her in a creek where she had never been before. We were not sure which the creek was, only knowing it from the landward side.

M. and I were to go out together and P. came to show us where he had left the punt. High tide was at dawn, and as the punt was so high up the creek we must embark at dawn. There was a fog, but, as there had been a fog on the previous day and it had cleared early in the morning, I thought this would clear later and we decided to go.

We went down the creek to the salting's edge and lay there waiting for the fog to clear sufficiently to allow us to cruise up the edge of the grass. We could hear many birds ; a small lot of brent geese to our left and a bigger lot further out, some wigeon to our right and, every now and then, the roar of a million wings as a large flock of waders changed its position. But, instead of clearing, the fog grew thicker.

The tide dropped so far that we would have been unable to go along the salting edge even if it had cleared. We must either abandon hope and go home now or go on and stay out for the whole day, until the tide allowed us to come in again in the evening. We decided to stay out, and so dropped down with the tide as the mud began to show. Visibility was reduced to within a gunshot, so whenever we moved down our creek we did so lying down and with the gun cocked and ready. However, we saw nothing except waders and gulls. Brent and wigeon were quite close to us on various occasions, we heard them but never saw them. Once we left our creek and went out over the flat mud in pursuit of the noise of brents, but they became quiet and we never found them.

When our little creek joined a big wide one,

we were unable to recognize it. Each of us thought it was a different place. However, we must wait here for the tide to drop further, so I decided to walk out over the mud to find out where we were. Taking the compass I set off to the west and walked for over a mile before reaching the next creek. This gave me the required information, as there could be only one stretch of creekless mud in the neighbourhood. I found my way back to the punt, with ease, by following my own tracks over the mud and taking a compass course over the sand where I had left no tracks. Not many years before, a shore shooter was drowned by the flowing tide on this very bank. He had no compass and got lost in the fog. I always try to take a compass whenever I leave the salting's edge, whether on my feet or in a boat; and I look upon two compasses as being a necessary part of the gear for any double punt.

As I neared the place where I had left the punt I heard a single pink-footed goose flying towards me. Then came the bang of M's gun and the splash as the goose fell in the creek.

The tide had ebbed enough by this time, so we set off once more. Aided by the strong current we passed swiftly down the bed of the creek. Redshanks looked like curlews and curlews like ostriches as they suddenly loomed out of the fog. We saw no ducks of any kind, only waders and gulls. The creek grew wider and wider until we could no longer see both sides at the same time. We would go down one side and then cross to the other whenever we thought we were nearing the places which we knew the duck preferred.

Then we heard wigeon ahead of us and pushed straight for the sound, taking the compass direction in case the sound should cease. Whenever there was a lull in the noise, M. watched the compass and directed me how to push. The birds sounded close to us, but I pushed a long way without seeing them. Then suddenly they appeared in front of us, still some way off apparently. When I could see them clearly I took out the glasses to see if they were worth shooting at, because they did not look very good to me. I was on the point of telling M. not to fire unless the two bunches went together, when he fired.

The smoke hung in the foggy atmosphere, and we could see nothing. I pushed on through the smoke, thinking that it was a very poor shot. As we emerged from the smoke I saw we had got some, then I saw we had got quite a lot, and then I suddenly realized that we had made a really good shot. M. took the punt after the few birds in the water, while I went ashore.

The fog was very kind to us and thinned round us while we were collecting the cripples. I hurriedly finished off those that might reach the water, then rounded up those which were running off into the fog. The mud was very soft and wet and so was I, by the time I had collected all our birds. When M. had got all those from the water, he went in the direction in which the flock had flown, to look for droppers. He got two, but a black-backed gull had eaten one of them before he reached it. We counted them over and found we had forty-two.

When we had finished stowing the birds, cleaned up the punt, and had some lunch, the tide was flowing again. The fog was just as thick as ever so we decided to let the tide flow up for some time, then follow the edge of it up the channel which we had come down, and on the high water to strike out along the edge of the shore. We saw nothing of great interest until we started along the shore in the evening. Then we came on several parties of wigeon and mallard besides many shellducks; but they were all on the water and too scattered for a shot. We neither saw nor heard any brent geese or knots. We did come on one party of pink-footed geese, but they saw us and swam away from us just as fast as we pursued them. It was late in the evening and very dark when we reached our moorings, close to where we had left the car. We had had a great shot, but it was entirely by luck and not by any great display of skill.

On this particular piece of coast, there are more mallards than I have ever seen elsewhere. One of their favourite resting places is on the top of a very large flat mudbank, where there are no creeks. We have tried many ways of approaching them, but none with any success. An ebb-tide would leave the punt high and dry in a few minutes, while a flood tide reaches the birds before the water is deep enough to float a punt. By the time the punt can get within range, the mallards are always swimming and scattered. If they are disturbed from this bank, they often go out to the open water. From a distance, when they are on the water, they look like a dense mass ; but a close approach shows them to be very scattered and not worth a shot.

If they are left undisturbed when they are on the water they often swim in and land on the edge of the sand. Here they often sit well, and, if the tide is not ebbing too fast, a punt can get within range. The best shot we ever made at them was twenty-six.

Mallard very rarely sit as closely packed as wigeon, and they usually see a punt before wigeon do, so a big shot at mallard is exceptional. If either mallard or pintail are mixed with wigeon, it is seldom that the wigeon are first to see the punt. Shellducks are the worst offenders of all, though we never shoot them they are very wild and always give the alarm. Herons, cormorants, curlews, and gulls are all much addicted to spoiling the punter's stalks. I have had a stalk spoiled by a seal and another spoiled by a salmon.

The greater black-backed gulls are perhaps the most mischievous of all. Once they have had a taste of a crippled wigeon they learn to associate the punt with a good meal, and will follow it for hours. But when a stalk is in progress they are not content to follow, but must go on ahead and swoop at the wigeon to put them up so that they may see if there are any cripples. If a pair of these gulls really get this habit firmly fixed, then it is well worth spending a day trying to shoot them. The best way of getting them is to find some good concealment and hide there, having previously shot a gull of any species. When the black-back shows himself in the distance, wave the corpse of the gull. If he sees it, he will come closer. When he is about 150 yards away, throw the corpse as high in the air as possible, and so that it will fall in the open. The black-back, if it does not already know the trick, will swoop straight down to see what is wrong with the other gull. Then is your chance

to polish him off, and perhaps use his corpse to
attract the attention of his mate, and so deal
with her. Sometimes a stone tied up in a white
handkerchief will work as well as a dead gull.

Herons, cormorants, curlews, and other birds
do not deliberately go out of their way to spoil
sport. If the punt happens to pass close to them
they frighten the ducks by their calls or their
frightened aspect.   But the result is just as
annoying, whether it was done with malice
aforethought, or not. On consulting my diary
I find that one day I had four stalks to fowl, all
spoiled;   first by a heron, then by swans, then
jackdaws, and lastly by swans and jackdaws
combined. Next day I went out with a single
punt and had stalks spoiled on various occasions
in the one morning by gulls, curlews, shellduck,
jackdaws, redshank, and a salmon. The swans
did not spoil any stalks that morning because
we had dealt with them in the dark of the previous
evening. In that place the swans had increased
and multiplied to such an extent that they were
ruining the Zostera which should have provided
the winter food for the wigeon. The harm is not
done by what the swans eat, but by what they pull
up by the roots. The salmon did his bit of dirty
work by jumping alongside the punt and falling
flat with a great slapping splash, just as I was
getting within range.

Curlews, when they are in sufficient quantities, are fair game for the puntsman. But it is a pity to shoot them unless they can be disposed of to people who will eat them. There are few parts of the coast where the people are not glad of a present of curlews. The moment when they present the best chance for a shot is when they have been driven up together by a high, flowing tide. After a few more minutes they may be washed off their legs and so fly inland to the fields. To make a successful shot the right moment must be chosen ; before that moment the birds are scattered about, and after it they have flown away. However, curlews usually choose the same place to rest on, every tide, so it is fairly simple to select the right moment for a stalk.

One such resting place is a long rocky shore with a small point of rocks jutting out into the bay. The curlews sit on this point which some-times looks all a golden brown colour, so many birds pack together there. One afternoon, in bright sunshine, we waited for our chance. We lay in the punt on the other side of the little bay, so that we could manœuvre into the position which seemed most suitable. The curlews all came and massed on their point, while we watched and waited for the best moment. But down the shore to the left was a little cliff, on which sat some jackdaws, while up the shallow shore to the right was an old heron. Both jackdaws and heron were more than likely to give us away, so we wondered what to do. Then we realized that by going straight across the bay to the curlews, we should have the sun behind us. The sun was low and there seemed a good chance that we should not be noticed coming straight from the eye of the sun.

The water would be deep most of the way so T. would have to scull. However, he was an excellent sculler, and the fastest I have ever seen. He had evolved a method which I have never seen used by anyone else. He had the longest and whippiest oar I have ever seen. Once the blade was ' biting ' the water, he could lie on his back and scull with his hands right down on his chest, the oar bending like a bow so that the blade was well down in the water. By using both hands he imparted great strength to each stroke. The great disadvantage of this method of sculling is that one must keep going. If one stops, or goes slow, or makes a mistake the oar no longer bites the water and so straightens itself and the blade comes right out of the water. This entails the lifting of a hand high above the punt to get the blade back in the water again. But the great advantage is that, if all goes well, the sculling arm is not visible to the fowl. With the ordinary method of sculling, the arm which does the work is in full view of the birds and is performing a very visible motion.

On this occasion all went well. T. sent the punt through the water almost as fast as if he were pushing with a setting pole. Only a very occasional word from me was necessary to keep the direction right, because, as he lay on his back, he could see the sun straight behind us. He could also see a cloud approaching the sun, and realized that if it covered the brilliant glare before we were within range, we should probably be seen by the fowl. The renewed energy and the stream of invective, produced by the sight of the cloud, made the punt tear through the water. We quickly came in range and I laid the gun on the nearest birds. Then we came in range of the thickest part, swung left, and aimed at them. In a few more yards we were out of the eye of the sun from the nearest birds. As they saw us and the first wings opened, which I could see out of the corner of my eye, I fired. The pandemonium of these thousands of startled, screaming whaups was almost deafening. Our pound of shot had cut a clean lane through the flock, killing forty-eight birds.

That same day we saw an extraordinary sight. As the punt slipped quietly round a rocky point we came on some mallards sitting amongst the seaweed and rocks. In such a position mallards are extremely difficult to see, so I looked at them through the glasses. There were only five grouped round a low, weed-covered post. Then the post turned its head and its great, brilliant yellow eyes looked straight at me. It was a short-eared owl, and it was sitting within 3 feet of the nearest mallards. What it was doing, sitting on the wet seaweed, I cannot imagine.

The short-eared owl is a bird which I have seen very often while shore shooting, but only on one other occasion have I seen it from a punt. Then we were lying waiting for the moon to rise. The tide was to be a very high one and the moon should rise about three-quarters of an hour before high water. We had got to the west of about two thousand pink-footed geese, so that the rising moon would show behind them and we should see them silhouetted against the light. While it was dark the geese kept very quiet, only giving an occasional call which kept us informed of their whereabouts. As the light improved with the nearing moon, the owl came flying along the tide edge. It saw us in the punt; perhaps it was attracted by our white sandwich paper. It hovered over us and wheeled round us, then would go away for a few minutes, only to return and try to make out what we were.

When we started off after the geese, the owl

took another look at us, but now we were moving it did not like us very much. On coming up to the geese we found them very scattered about. Two or three times we might have made a nice little shot at them, but we did not want to disturb such a large flock of geese except for a really good shot. The dark western sky was behind us, so we were able to cruise about and look at the different scattered parties without disturbing them. None of them offered a really good chance, so we retreated again quietly, only disturbing one small party which went off and settled with the others.

Our method with these geese was to punt only to small parties of them, and never to the big flocks of over one hundred unless there was a good chance of making a big shot. By this means we often got six or seven birds and only frightened a few others. Had we shot off at the big lots for the sake of getting six or seven we would have frightened them and so spoiled our sport for a long time. It is always best to wait until fowl give a good opportunity before even letting them see a punt. If one should approach fowl of any species and disturb them and, for some reason not have a shot at them, it is as well to remain lying still in the bottom of the punt until they have all cleared right away. The apparition of a man suddenly rising from the low punt must be much more startling to the fowl than is the sight of the punt itself. If they see their arch enemy suddenly appear like this, they must learn to associate the punt with danger, whereas if they do not see man they may not realize that the punt has anything to do with him.

Chapter XIII

ON THE TESTING OF PUNT GUNS

Since writing most of this book, I have tried out two punt guns at a target, in order to test their pattern and find out their ranges, etc. Both these guns have performed well in practical fowling. So far as I am aware the only person who has tested punt guns at a target, and published his results, is Sir Ralph Payne-Gallwey. He published these results in the *Shooting (Moor and Marsh)* volume of the Badminton Library.

Many wildfowlers state that it is quite un-necessary to try a punt gun at a target, asserting that wildfowl are a good enough target to test the gun. I entirely disagree. By firing a big gun at a target it is possible to find out what is the fault, if any. By firing it at fowl it is possible to find out if there is a fault, but it is nearly impossible to say what is the fault.

One wildfowler of my acquaintance, belonging to the school of thought which dislikes target trials, had a gun which he said 'shot soft'. To counteract the alleged 'softness' he increased his powder charge and reduced his shot. I went out with his gun and experienced the most

THE SHOT

lamentable series of bad shots. Then, finding a steep mudbank, I had a shot at it. His gun, which fired 14 oz of shot, had a pattern of 18 feet diameter at 50 yards !

That evening I loaded some cartridges for him. I increased the shot a great deal and decreased the powder in the requisite proportion. I also used more than twice as much wadding as he had used. The prophets asserted that the shot would merely trickle out of the end of the barrel. However, we tried the cartridge at birds and made a beautiful shot, cutting a line of cleanly killed birds straight through the middle of a flock of curlews. A proper target trial would probably have suggested an even better load. A trial when the gun was first bought would have saved the owner two seasons of fruitless bird scaring. He would have found that, instead of ' shooting soft ', the overdose of powder was scattering his small charge of shot ; also that the small quantity of wadding was apparently blowing through the shot.

The trials which I have just made are by no means complete. Lack of time prevented further trials with different loads. These I hope to make in the near future ; and I am confident of being able to improve the pattern of the smaller gun, without reducing the penetration, while it may be possible to improve that of the larger gun.

I will give full details of the trials for the benefit of anyone who wishes to try his own gun. We secured five sheets of 9 ft corrugated iron, two 12 ft beams of 4 in by 2 in deal, and the requisite number of bolts and nuts. Bolting the sheets of iron to the beams, one at top and one at bottom, we made a target 9 feet high and 10 feet wide. We then took this target, two 13 ft props, an anchor and rope and a bucket of whitewash and brush, out on to the sands at the edge of the channel.

The target would have caught the wind and been blown over, if allowed to ; so we buried the anchor in the sand behind the target and tied the rope from the anchor to the top of the target, making it of such a length that the target was upright when the rope was taught. This prevented it from falling forwards, and the two props were set behind the target to prevent it from falling backwards. Before each shot the target was whitewashed and a piece of wet newspaper placed in the middle as an aiming mark. Each pellet mark was plainly visible on the whitewash. The props were taken away and the target lowered backwards, to facilitate the whitewashing and the counting of pellets.

One of my chief reasons for wishing to try the guns was to find out the ideal range and the maximum range. People talk, and I have talked myself, of firing at 120 yards. I believe that no one ever does fire successfully at such a range. Set up some dead ducks on the sand, walk away for 120, or even 100 yards, then, with eyes at the level which they would be in a punt, look at the ducks : you would no more think of shooting at them than you would think of kicking them, so far away do they appear to you if you have had any practical experience of punt gunning. But there are days of clear atmosphere and brilliant sunshine, when birds do appear to be very much closer than they are, and on such days I have made the mistake of firing at ranges up to 150 yards, which of course is far above the maximum range. To the novice, birds on open water, sand, or mud always look much closer than they really are.

We first tried my punt gun of 2 in bore, with a charge of 2 lb of shot and 6¼ oz of powder. The wadding between powder and shot consisted of, first a linoleum wad, then 2 oz of tightly rammed oakum, then another linoleum wad. The ignition was provided by a ·380 blank revolver cartridge. This was the load which we have been using with great success for some years.

Two shots were fired at 100 yards' distance from the target and averaged 195 pellets of BB

in a circle of 6 ft diameter. The whole target
was hit in every corner, the pattern was very
even but very open and not nearly good enough
for killing fowl. Also the penetration left much
to be desired.

Two shots were fired at 100 yards, loaded
with AAA. These averaged 177 pellets in the
6 ft circle. The worst of the two had only
133 pellets in the 6 ft circle, but the pattern was
even and of the same density throughout the
10 ft circle, while the penetration was excellent.
We had the impression that this shot would have
killed very much better than either of the previous
ones loaded with BB.

The better of the two AAA shots had 524
pellets in the 10 ft circle, of which 348 were in
the 8 ft circle, of which 221 were in the 6 ft
circle. The whole pattern was very even and
the penetration was very good.

The conclusions which we arrived at from
these shots at 100 yards range were as follows.

Firstly, a shot at so great a range is to be
avoided with this gun : it is too far. But that
if a cartridge is fired at 100 yards it should be
loaded with AAA rather than BB. Such a
charge of AAA would be moderately effective
against geese but the pattern would be too open
for ducks. It would be most unsporting to
fire even AAA at this range, because many

birds would be wounded. An increase of the shot charge and a corresponding decrease of the powder charge would probably produce a better pattern and still retain sufficient penetration.

Bringing the punt to 80 yards from the target we fired two more shots loaded with BB. The pattern and penetration of both these shots was good, and gave an average of 585 pellets in the 6 ft circle. The pattern was only slightly less dense in the 10 ft circle. Both these shots would have been effective against ducks or geese. We concluded from them that 80 yards was the maximum effective range of this gun, and that BB gave ample penetration at this range.

We were left wondering what had happened to all the other pellets in the charge. Where had they gone and why had they gone there? We searched about and found many pellets that had hit the soft sand or the shallow pools. All were so badly misshapen that it was difficult to imagine that they had ever been round. Each individual pellet had been compressed by each of its neighbours so that the best of them were irregular and twelve sided, while some of the worst were of such a shape that they baffled description. Their line of flight must have been like that of a boomerang. The pellets which had hit the target were very flattened, but, in spite of that, we could see that they had been those which were least badly misshapen. It is obvious that the spherical shot must travel straightest, and that the harder the shot is, the more it is likely to remain spherical; therefore the hardest procurable shot will give the best pattern.

Our next trial was with a gun of $1\frac{1}{2}$ in bore, with a charge of 20 oz of shot and 3 oz of powder. The wadding between powder and shot consisted of two felt wads.

At 80 yards, two cartridges loaded with BB averaged 208 pellets in the 6 ft circle. Both patterns were patchy, the shot being in little groups and not evenly distributed. Both patterns were inclined to ' cart wheel '; leaving the centre of the pattern clean and placing the shot in a circle round it. We concluded that neither of these shots would have been effective against fowl.

We then fired the same gun, loaded with the same charge, at 70 yards from the target. This gave 322 pellets in the 6 ft circle. This pattern was still patchy and inclined to ' cart wheel ', so would have produced many wounded birds.

Two shots fired at 60 yards from the target gave an average of 400 pellets in the 6 ft circle. Both shots would have been effective against fowl.

We drew the following conclusions from the tests of this second gun : That 60 yards was the

maximum effective range for that load. That the
load had one or all of these faults ; too much
powder, too little shot, or inefficient wadding.
As I have already stated, lack of time prevented
the trial of different loads. Personally I think
the wadding was the trouble. I have always
found oakum better than felt.

Another object of these tests was to find out
the exact sighting for the correct placing of the
centre of the pattern, at various ranges. After
finding the height of back-sight required I
evolved the shape of back-sight which is here
figured :—

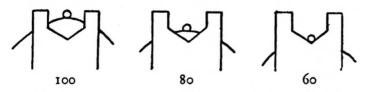

100   80   60

With this sight the correct aim can be taken
at any range, without having to alter or adjust
the sight. In actual practice, when the punt
draws to within 100 yards of the fowl the gun
is aimed so that the bead of the foresight is in
line with the top of the back-sight. When 80 yards
is reached the bead of the foresight is brought in
line with the shoulders of the V. At 60 yards the
bead is at the bottom of the V.

I hope, by using this sight, to make correct
aiming more ' fool-proof '. Both my friends and

I have so often had our aiming instructions
misunderstood by some of the novices whom
we have taken out punting. Most novices, and even
some old hands, seem to think that a punt gun
merely needs to be pointed in the direction of
the fowl. When they see a back-sight which is
not unlike that of a rifle they realize that a punt
gun is not such an enormous scatter gun as
they had thought.

The actions of a punt gun, when fired, are
not generally known. They are too quick to be
seen by the human eye which has blinked shut

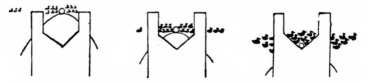

at the report of the explosion. From photographs
and a cinema film, I have seen this action. First,
the gun recoils straight back against the
breeching rope, the muzzle rising slightly at the
same time. Then the breeching rope, which
has been stretched tight, contracts and throws
the gun forward, making the muzzle rise still
further. Then the barrel falls with a crash on to
the gun rest. Hence the reason for having a
well-padded top to the rest. The illustration
facing page 242 shows the gun being thrown
forward by the contraction of the breeching rope,
this shot having been fired almost horizontally.

INDEX

A

Accident with gunpowder, 194
Action of punt gun when fired, 250
Amberite, 15
Ammunition box, 187, 188
Anchor, 207–210
Anorak, 32
Aster, Sea, 140

B

Back sight for punt gun, 249–250
Bad cartridges, 18
Baling tin, 210
Balance of punt gun, 174
Barrel, as a butt, 37
Bats, 163
Bean Goose, 82, 86, 115, 223
Bean Geese, Punting to, 220–4
Bedding, Dogs, 50
Bernacle Geese, 62, 216
Bernacle geese, Shooting, 104–111
Black backed gulls, 110
Black backs, how to lure, 234
Boat, shooting from, 21
Bootjack recoil board, 170, 174
Boots, 25
Boots, drying rubber, 26
Breeches of punt guns, 168, 169
Breeching rope, 171–4
   ,,   ,,   breaking, 172, 173.
Butts, 37
   ,, position of, 148

C

Canvas hides, 37
Cap, 26
Caps, percussion, 197
Cartridges, 13–19
Cartridge belt, 28
   ,,   extractor, 28
Cartridges, punt gun, 189–195
Cleaning guns, 22, 23
Cleats, 204
Coat, 26
Collecting birds, 80
Compass, 33
Corrals for cripple catching, 129–130
Cripple stopper cartridges, 188
Crutch for punt gun, 175, 176
Curlew, Punting to, 236–8
Curlew shooting, 64–77

D

Decoys, 34–7
Dogs, 41–54
   ,, Breeds of, 41, 42
Dog, care of, 50
Dog collar, danger of, 54
Dog, training to water, 44
   ,, punting, 47, 48
Driving greylags, 102
Drying boots, 26
Ducks resting place for, 127
Duck shooting, 131–164

E

Elevator for punt gun, 176–9

Lightning Source UK Ltd.
Milton Keynes UK
11 March 2010

151248UK00001B/16/P